EDUCATING INEQUALITY

Politicians and school officials often contend that higher education is the solution to many of our social and economic problems. *Educating Inequality* argues that in order to reduce inequality and enhance social mobility, public policies are needed to revamp the financial aid system and increase the number of good jobs. Exploring topics such as the fairness of the current social system, the focus on individual competition in an unequal society, and democracy and capitalism in higher education, this important book seeks to uncover the major myths that shape how people view higher education and its relation to the economy. Looking to models that generate economic mobility and social equality, this book advocates a broader vision for public higher education to promote universal equality and global awareness.

Robert Samuels is a Lecturer in the Writing Program at the University of California, Santa Barbara, USA.

EDUCATING INEQUALITY

Beyond the Political Myths of Higher
Education and the Job Market

Robert Samuels

NEW YORK AND LONDON

First published 2018
by Routledge
711 Third Avenue, New York, NY 10017

and by Routledge
2 Park Square, Milton Park, Abingdon, Oxon, OX14 4RN

Routledge is an imprint of the Taylor & Francis Group, an informa business

© 2018 Taylor & Francis

The right of Robert Samuels to be identified as author of this work has been asserted by him in accordance with sections 77 and 78 of the Copyright, Designs and Patents Act 1988.

All rights reserved. No part of this book may be reprinted or reproduced or utilised in any form or by any electronic, mechanical, or other means, now known or hereafter invented, including photocopying and recording, or in any information storage or retrieval system, without permission in writing from the publishers.

Trademark notice: Product or corporate names may be trademarks or registered trademarks, and are used only for identification and explanation without intent to infringe.

Library of Congress Cataloging-in-Publication Data
A catalog record for this book has been requested

ISBN: 978-1-138-06897-1 (hbk)
ISBN: 978-1-138-08498-8 (pbk)
ISBN: 978-1-315-11158-2 (ebk)

Typeset in New Baskerville
by codeMantra

CONTENTS

Preface   ix

1   The Politics of Higher Education   1
Class without Class 1
The Bipartisan Support of the Education Solution 4
The Gold Star Fallacy 6
Beyond Political Myths 9

2   College and the Myth of the Good Job   12
Degree Deflation 13
The Academic Lottery Economy 13
The STEM Degree Myth 15
Why Politicians Believe in Education Myths 19
The Mismatch Myth 20
Producing Underemployment 25
The Middle-Class Myth 27
The Poor Get Poorer through Higher Education 30

3   Why Higher Education Reduces Social Mobility?   37
Poor Students with Cadillacs 38
How the Private Became Public 39
Generating Poverty through Aid 41
From Need to Merit 43
The Work-Study Myth 44
Tax Welfare for the Wealthy 45
Ripping Off Vets 46

CONTENTS

The Myth of Need-Blind Admissions 47
Separate and Unequal 49
A Fairer Model for Financial Aid 50

4 The Myth of the Fair Meritocracy   55
Higher Education's Anti-meritocracy 55
Experimenting with Meritocracy 57
Rationalizing Inequality 62
The Ideology of Meritocracy 63
Sorting vs. Learning 65

5 How College Changed Childhood, Education, and
Parenting in America   68
Beating the Birth Lottery 68
The College-Parenting Complex 69
Meritocratic Parenting and Educating 73
The Culture of Meritocratic Parenting 89

6 Training Undemocratic Capitalists   101
Ranking the Rankings 103
Doing College 105
College Life against Critical Thinking 107
Paying for Class 108
Drinking Not Thinking 112
Joining Exclusivity 114

7 The Death of the Liberal Classroom   118
Values vs. Actions 119
Institutional Suicide 120
Conservative Science 126
The Computer Brain 127
The Politics of Brain Science 128
The Libertarian Web 130
Education, the Web, and New Social Darwinism 131
Invasion of the Massive Open Online Course 135

CONTENTS   vii

8   Will Technology and the Free Market Save Higher
    Ed and the Job Market?   142
    Post-recession Massive Open Online Courses 143
    The Darwinian Innovation Myth 148
    The Darwinian University 151
    The MOOC Myth 154
    The Free Market Solution 162

    Conclusion – Educating Equality   167
    Democracy and Capitalism 168
    *Making Higher Education More Democratic and
        Less Capitalistic 172*

    Index   177

PREFACE

After writing *Why Public Higher Education Should Be Free*, I had the opportunity to talk to many people who are concerned about the current plight of our nation's colleges and universities. During these discussions with government officials, students, parents, and faculty, I kept on encountering the same set of misunderstandings, and so I decided to write this book to clear up the major myths that shape how people view the important topic of higher education and its relation to the economy. As I argue in Chapter 1, politicians often claim that higher education is the main path to a middle-class job, but by presenting college as the key to economic advancement, they often avoid addressing many of the sources of our economic woes: de-unionization, outsourcing, financialization, taxation, profit-hording, and automation. This book argues that college degrees do not create good jobs, and without the production of more good jobs, an increasing number of students will go into debt in order to compete for a smaller number of well-compensated positions. The solution is to make college affordable and accessible, while we develop policies to reduce inequality and enhance social mobility.

One of the main myths about higher education is the idea that the best way to produce better jobs is to have more people with bachelor degrees. According to this logic, since people with college degrees make more money on average, if more people attain degrees, then everyone will be wealthier. As Chapter 2 shows, this myth is misleading because many recent college graduates are not working at jobs that traditionally require a college degree, and most of the advantage that college students have in lifetime earnings is due to the decrease in wages for people without college degrees. Moreover, contrary to popular belief, there is a very loose relation between particular degrees and future jobs. In fact, more than half of the people working in STEM (science, technology, engineering, and math) jobs do not have STEM degrees, and more than half of the people with STEM degrees are not working in STEM jobs. It therefore makes no sense for us to focus on having more students graduate with a particular major. It is also clear that the main reason for high rates of underemployment is not that people are not trained in the right areas; the problem is that there are not enough well-paying jobs to support a growing middle class.

Not only does attaining a college degree no longer necessarily lead to a good job, but as Chapter 3 shows, higher education now often increases inequality and decreases social mobility. Due to the way we fund and pay for college, wealthy students tend to go to rich schools with high graduation rates, while low-income students usually go to low-funded schools with low graduation rates. The result is that after spending trillions of dollars on financial aid over the last forty years, we have seen a dramatic increase in the number of upper-income students with college degrees and little improvement in degree attainment for low- and middle-income students. Thus, counter to the myth that higher education increases social mobility and reduces inequality, the opposite is now the case.

As Chapter 4 shows, people still think that higher education is the key to individual economic advancement and social equality because they believe that higher education is a fair meritocracy. In fact, this myth is the main source for the general belief that if you just work hard and play by the rules, you will be rewarded for your talent and effort. According to this meritocratic myth, unlike aristocratic societies that are structured by inherited wealth and power, our society rewards people based on their proven abilities. However, a careful analysis of the role played by SAT scores in higher education shows that since these

PREFACE xi

meritocratic tests are highly correlated with wealth, the meritocracy has reverted back to an aristocracy. SAT tests are supposed to be a fair and objective way of judging knowledge, but students coming from wealthy families have huge advantages due to their previous education, the education of their parents, access to test training, and a whole set of privileges derived from wealth inequality.

This book argues that in order to promote higher education *and* a more just and equal social system, we need public policies that revamp our financial aid system and increase the number of good jobs. In fact, to provide a more even playing field for higher education, the wealth of the students and their parents should not determine who enrolls and graduates from college. Yet, we need to combine this change in how schools are funded and supported with a change in how jobs are created and maintained. Luckily, as I discuss at the end of this book, there are models in Northern Europe detailing how to generate economic mobility and social equality. In fact, in Germany and most Scandinavian countries, free public higher education is combined with a low level of income inequality, high economic productivity, and a fortified middle class. However, the United States will never attain this level of social fairness if it does not first give up on the myths that make higher education the main solution to economic inequality.

This focus on seeing college as the only solution to individual and national economic advancement is explored in Chapter 5, where I examine the ways childhood, parenting, and K-12 education have been reshaped by the pressure to get into a "good" university. As society becomes more unequal and the rewards for attending an elite college increase, parents concentrate on doing everything they can to help their kids outcompete other children. The end result is that society becomes more competitive and unequal as possible social solutions are ignored. Here, we see what happens when a public good turns into a private good, and everyone seeks to outcompete everyone else for a reduced scarce resource.

This focus on individual competition in an unequal society is further explored in Chapter 6, where I show how, through its use of large lecture classes, reductive multiple-choice exams, and competitive grading systems, higher education often fails to teach critical thinking or democratic citizenship. In fact, the obsession over rating, ranking, and grading everything reveals an ideological bias that blinds us from understanding the complexity of human experience, as we end up socializing students to be undemocratic capitalists.

If higher education now increases inequality and trains people to be disengaged competitors, we have to ask why universities are still considered to be liberal institutions. In Chapter 7, I answer this question by explaining both the reasons behind the conservative attack on higher education and the self-defeating practices and policies of liberal professors and administrators. What we find is that liberal institutions, like higher education, have been undermined by a focus on individual careerism and a fear of any real radical progressive change.

Since many liberal faculties have not fought for a more just and fair system, they have opened the door for conservatives to offer regressive ways of changing higher education. As I depict in Chapter 8, Republicans and libertarians often argue that the best way to make college more affordable and effective is to turn to the free market and new technological advances. Thus, from this perspective, college is expensive because public universities do not have to compete for resources and funding; in fact, schools can raise tuition because they know that the government will give financial aid and loans to cover the increased cost. However, we know from the recent history of for-profit colleges that these free market schools have increased tuition and lowered educational quality as they spend most of their money on marketing and administration. Moreover, many of these colleges do use online education as a new form of technological disruption, but the result is usually a reduction in student learning and completion.

PREFACE

xiii

The conclusion to this book points to a way out of this ideological trap. Not only do we have to make higher education affordable and accessible but also we have to help students and parents to see that higher education is more than just job preparation. By turning higher education back into a public good instead of a private good, we can begin the process of reversing the decades long ideological battle to demonize government, welfare programs, teachers, unions, job security, and state regulations. Part of this effort will require moving beyond the current liberal and conservative consensus that higher education is the solution to all of our problems during a time when public universities and colleges are being systematically defunded and wage and income inequality continues to increase.

It is my hope that this book will help parents, students, citizens, and governmental officials take on a more realistic view of how higher education relates to the job market. Parents, in particular, have to realize that by turning education into a system of meritocratic competition, everyone ends up losing. It is therefore necessary for all of us to understand the myths shaping our vision of employment, inequality, and education. As an example of critical university studies, this work intends to help academic researchers place higher education in a larger social and political context.

1

THE POLITICS OF HIGHER EDUCATION

Politicians and school officials often argue that higher education is the central solution to many of our social and economic problems; however, at the same moment that college is supposed to reduce inequality and increase social mobility, we find that the opposite is often the case. The focus of this chapter is on the political reasons for positioning higher education as the cure for inequality and poverty. By examining a set of related myths concerning degrees, jobs, and inequality, we will see how politicians often misrepresent the economic effects of higher education.

Class without Class

In his book, *Class Dismissed*, John Marsh traces the history of the myth that higher education solves the problem of inequality.[1] As Marsh highlights, one of the earlier proponents of higher education as the solution to economic issues was Andrew Carnegie, who is known for his generous giving to libraries and universities. What most people do not know is that at the same moment that he was donating a great deal of wealth, he was also doing everything he could to stop workers from unionizing.[2] Not only did Carnegie oppose the minimum wage and laws regulating working hours, but he also believed that any form of charitable aid would make workers lazy and dependent. However, he did think that wealthy people should give money to educational institutions because he believed that aid leading to personal betterment is superior to support for people who have not shown that they are hard working.[3]

Marsh unearths here an interesting dynamic regarding wealth, education, and inequality that still exists today: people resist giving governmental support or even charity to people who do not appear to be trying to better themselves. Thus, while many other countries have a more robust social safety net, America tends to use education as one of the main ways of dealing with poverty and economic inequality. In fact, like Carnegie, many Americans believe that wealthy people deserve their wealth because they have worked hard for it, and since in the land of equal opportunity, anyone can become wealthy, then it must be the fault of the poor if they cannot afford to live on their own.[4] Moreover, as Marsh reveals, education in general, and increasingly higher education, is seen as the main system of equal opportunity and advancement.

This preference for education over direct intervention in the labor market turned out to be one of the key aspects of President Johnson's War on Poverty strategy. As he told Sargent Shriver, "We don't want any doles."[5] In other words, they did not want to just give people money to help them escape the ravages of poverty; they also did not think that creating jobs through government programs would work because they believed that there were already enough employment opportunities. In short, Johnson and his advisors thought that the problem was that the poor just didn't have the skills or the will to compete in the labor system. In order to correct this deficit in the "culture of poverty," the Johnson administration believed that support for education, housing, medical care, and training would give poor people a fair chance in a fair system. Although these were important and needed programs, Marsh points out that this stress on using education and training to prepare people for jobs placed the blame for poor people's plight on their own lack of skills. At one point, Johnson is quoted as saying: "The answer for all our national problems comes down to one single word: education."[6] Here we see how one of the greatest American efforts to create a more equal society was led by a man who thought that education could solve all social problems.

THE POLITICS OF HIGHER EDUCATION   3

As Marsh convincingly shows, the only policy that has really reduced the poverty level in America and other countries is government programs that directly transfer money to the poor. For instance, the great reduction of poverty rates in America occurred between the late 1960s and the early 1970s, and during this time, we saw the implementation of public policies like food stamps, Medicare, Medicaid, and supplemental security income.[7] Marsh reports that in 1972, these programs lifted half of the people in poverty over the poverty line.[8] Thus, even though Americans tend to reject any program that simply gives poor people aid, it turns out that these kinds of policies are the ones that not only help to reduce income inequality, but can also stimulate the economic growth by putting money into the hands of people who will spend it directly in the local economy.[9]

Since Americans tend to distrust any government program that does not make people work for their support, education is the preferred method for trying to help people escape from poverty. However, as we shall see, wealthy people tend to attend college and complete higher ed degrees at a much higher rate than low- and middle-income people, and so the stress on higher education as the solution to inequality does not work by itself. Of course, one reason why we cannot educate our way out of inequality is that degrees do not produce jobs, and short of creating government jobs for every unemployed or underemployed worker, the federal government has very little control over the private labor market. For instance, in the mid-1970s, between 32 and 38 million jobs disappeared in America.[10] These job losses were not due to workers suddenly not having enough education or skills; what happened was that in the face of global competition, companies decided to close down or outsource much of their production. Without any strong government intervention or direct support for displaced workers, the result was a massive increase in unemployment and a decrease in wages from which we have never really recovered.[11] In fact, the response to de-industrialization was often a governmental retreat, and the declaration that government was not part of the solution but somehow was the problem itself.[12]

4   THE POLITICS OF HIGHER EDUCATION

One of the major economic trends in the twentieth century was the relation between productivity and wages. Up until the mid-1970s, wages and productivity went up together, but starting in the 1970s, productivity quickly increased at a much faster rate than the wages of the average worker.[13] It is clear that one of the main causes for this divergence was that managers were keeping a larger percentage of the profits, but another problem was that workers had lost their bargaining power. As Marsh relates, in 1945, 34.5% of all wage earners were in a union, but by 1972, only 26.3% were organized, and in 2012, the rate was 12%.[14] Since the mid-1970s, fewer people are in unions, but more people are gaining college degrees, and one of the results is that the wages for most workers have remained flat. Clearly, education is not the main solution to this problem of growing wealth and income inequality.

The Bipartisan Support of the Education Solution

This desire to see higher education as the solution to inequality has been one of the only ideas that liberals and conservatives both support, and so it is interesting to look at why it crosses party lines. Marsh points out that in the case of Bill Clinton and many other new Democrats, the move was made to concentrate on supply-side issues rather than on demand-oriented policies concerning taxes and wages.[15] Tired of being seen as tax-and-spend liberals, these Democrats embraced policies like the North American Free Trade Agreement (NAFTA) and the deregulation of the financial markets.[16] Moreover, as parties on both sides of the aisle become increasingly dependent on large donors to fund their expensive campaigns, there was little stomach for anyone to try to regulate the companies that funded their campaigns.[17] Instead of confronting the issues of corporate greed, Republicans and Democrats turned to higher education as the explanation for why middle-class workers could no longer find secure, well-paying jobs. According to this bipartisan logic, Americans just didn't have the right education to compete in the new globalized economy. Of course, corporations also like the idea that they can reduce their own spending for training if the government helps universities and colleges provide the needed skills.[18]

Marsh adds that one reason why people believe that education is perhaps the best way for individuals to become wealthy is that it has worked out that way for many people, especially in the past. He also points out that as other paths for advancement have disappeared, higher education still remains one of the only routes for potential advancement.[19] Due, then, to the partial success of education in the past and the present, politicians have found it convenient to see education as both the problem and the solution. According to this bipartisan logic, since everyone wants to get ahead in life, and a college degree can help some advance, higher education is the best way to reduce economic inequality; however, when everyone strives after the same solution, and that solution is rationed, the result can only be more inequality.

Another related issue is that if we see higher education as the solution to social mobility and economic inequality, we focus our attention on the gains of particular individuals and not on the society as a whole. Here we see how a public good is transformed into a private good, which then undermines the public support for that good. Of course, the other side of this logic is that if people are not successful, it must be their own fault.

One reason why politicians from both parties buy into these myths is that these elected officials have almost all been successful products of the meritocratic system, and as Marsh adds, virtually none of them have been members of unions.[20] To prove the power of the ideology of meritocracy on the ruling class, he refers to a study indicating that people who have more education believe that more economic opportunity exists than does in reality. Moreover, these same people tend to oppose policies that would reduce income inequality because they believe that wealth is well earned, while poverty is well deserved.[21] In what he calls "the narcissism of meritocracy," people with the most education tend to deny the structural causes for inequality. In other words, people base their view of the world on their own experiences, and if higher education has helped them out financially, they believe it is the answer for everyone else.

As Marsh stresses, higher education allows some people to sleep at night because they believe that we have a fair system of equal opportunity, and thus poor people have only themselves to blame.[22] However, while polls show that a large majority of Americans think that income and wealth should be more evenly distributed, virtually the same percentage of people disagree that it is the government's responsibility to reduce income inequality.[23] Interestingly, even a larger percentage of people think that the government should make sure that everyone who wants to go to college can attend. Thus, people are aware of the problems of inequality, but one of the only ways they think the government can help is by supporting higher education.

The desire to see higher education as the solution to social and economic inequality derives in part from the political myths of the invisible hand, the fair meritocracy, and social Darwinism. Underlying these beliefs about education and the economy is the simple idea that people are rewarded for their individual talents, and if people are given free aid, they will not work hard or try to improve themselves. In other words, part of the meritocratic myth is the notion that people get what they deserve, and what they deserve is what they earn on their own. Another related myth is that if people do not pay for something, they will not appreciate it, and so we must make people pay for their higher education.[24] In what is now called "putting skin in the game," a guiding assumption behind our public policies is that external rewards and payments are the only thing that really motivates people, and without these extrinsic motivations, people will revert to their default positions of doing the least possible for the biggest payoff. This belief in external rewards shapes how we structure our schools and how we view governmental policies.

The Gold Star Fallacy

Recent studies on motivation have challenged the idea that the best way to get people to do something or learn something is to give them an external reward. According to the study "Extrinsic Rewards and Intrinsic Motivation," external rewards can actually significantly reduce internal motivation.[25] In other words, the use of grades in education and bonuses in jobs often functions to produce cynical conformity and a lost sense of self-direction. For example, when teachers or employers use tangible external rewards, the receiver of the award sees control as being located outside of the self, and a sense of self-control and competence is diminished. Moreover, if someone is working merely to receive a reward, internal motivation is reduced further.

This theory regarding the power of external rewards to undermine internal motivation directly contradicts many of the myths that currently guide public opinion and governmental policies regarding education and employment. Since we believe that higher education is a fair meritocratic system that effectively awards people for their superior talents and accomplishments, we promote a survival of the fittest mentality, which also feeds into the myth of the invisible hand. Furthermore, people tend to believe that they are responsible for their accomplishments, but other external forces are to blame for their failures. On the other hand, we have a tendency to blame others for our problems. In fact, Mark Bracher, in his book *Social Symptoms and Identity Needs*, argues that a major reason why we cannot solve social problems like economic inequality is that we believe that people are poor because they have made individual bad decisions, and they have made these choices because they have a flawed character.[26] Bracher argues that we want to blame the poor for being poor and the unemployed for being unemployed because we want to maintain our identities as being good by locating a group of people who are bad.[27] By blaming and scapegoating the poor and the uneducated, we reinforce our sense of being good and right. In this sense, publicized standardized tests like the ones promoted by President Bush's No Child Left Behind and President Obama's Race to the Top serve the social and psychological function of clearly distinguishing

8 THE POLITICS OF HIGHER EDUCATION

between the worthy and the unworthy. Likewise, using college rankings in higher education also functions to sort institutions into winners and losers.

In order to break this cycle of blaming and shaming, we have to rethink higher education as a shared system and public good. Not only should we reduce the importance of ranking systems and grades, but we must also make the classroom a place of participation and collaboration.[28] However, as we have seen, these ideal goals are undermined by the stress on the isolated individual in all aspects of our culture. Furthermore, countries like the United States have been subjected to a very effective campaign to get people to stop believing that the government can fix large social problems. In fact, underlying the neoliberal libertarian ideology is the simple myth that you can only trust the people who are closest to you. As Richard Wilkinson and Kate Pickett argue in *The Spirit Level*, perhaps the biggest effect of high social and economic inequality is a loss of social trust: as people sort themselves into classes, each group has less contact with the other groups, and a lack of trust emerges.[29] Wilkinson and Pickett add that when the differences between the groups grow, social empathy breaks down, and people do not feel responsible for helping out people external to their own group.[30]

The problem, thus, is not only that our societies are becoming more unequal, but also that inequality is constantly being measured and publicized. Since people often judge their own value and worth in relation to the people around them, the educational ranking and rating of people and institutions only lead to a greater sense of mistrust and social isolation. In a vicious circle, the more a society becomes unequal, the more social trust decreases, and the more social trust decreases, the less societies want to do anything to decrease inequality.[31] From this perspective, one aspect of the conservative war on government and taxes is the promotion of policies that produce greater wealth inequality, which, in turn, reduces social trust and the belief that the government can fight inequality.

Beyond Political Myths

Throughout this book, I argue that the biggest problem that we face as a nation is that we believe in a series of myths that prevent us from using current resources in a more effective manner. Since we believe in the myth that education is the solution to all of our social and economic problems, we do not push for a wider range of public policies. Moreover, since we still idealize our meritocracy, we fail to see how our systems are being gamed by the wealthy. As inequality increases and job opportunities decrease, we have doubled down on the myth of higher education as the solution.

As our democratic system and our economy become more undemocratic, people retreat into a set of myths that can be understood through the concepts of neoliberalism, libertarianism, and social Darwinism. The neoliberal myth argues that all public functions should be privatized, and we must impose austerity measures to reduce governmental functions. Libertarianism adds to this myth by insisting that taxes are, by nature, theft, and the free market is the ultimate form of human freedom. In a bipartisan effort, Ronald Reagan argued that the government is the problem and not the solution, and Bill Clinton added that "the era of big government is over."[32] This libertarian consensus goes hand in hand with the myth of social Darwinism, which states that our economic system is a mode of natural selection where only the strong survive. Moreover, inequality is then further enhanced by the myth of meritocracy that tells us that the sorting of the world into winners and losers is a fair way to run a society.

Even if people don't fully believe these myths, they have been socialized to live their lives in a mode of cynical conformity. In other words, people act as if these myths are true even when they doubt their validity, and underlying this cynicism is a loss of trust in our social systems and each other. While education should be a place where this trust is nourished, the reality is that we have a grading and sorting system that turns everyone into distrustful competitors. When we add the high level of personal debt that higher education is generating, universities and colleges no longer are places that give people a temporary opportunity to escape from the rigid logic of the market. People now often go to college to get a job and not to become critical thinkers and active citizens.

All of these trends can be reversed: after all, there is nothing natural or inevitable about the myths we use to structure our perceptions of our social worlds. Education should be a place where these myths are challenged and discussed, but the loss of faculty tenure and the standardization of education prevents teachers from confronting these belief systems. As the Right attacks universities for being bastions of liberal indoctrination, the Left often retreats to careerism and an investment in meritocratic inequality. The goal of this book, then, is to help uncover the myths that circulate on the Right and the Left about degrees, jobs, and inequality.

Notes

1 Marsh, John. *Class dismissed: Why we cannot teach or learn our way out of inequality.* NYU Press, 2011.
2 Ibid., 95–97.
3 96.
4 Zucker, Gail Sahar, and Bernard Weiner. "Conservatism and perceptions of poverty: An attributional analysis1." *Journal of Applied Social Psychology* 23.12 (1993): 925–943.
5 Marsh, 142.
6 147.
7 Ibid., 150.
8 Ibid., 151.
9 Krugman, Paul. *End this depression now!.* WW Norton & Company, 2012.
10 Marsh, 159.
11 Bluestone, Barry, and Bennett Harrison. "*The deindustrialization of America.*" (1982).
12 Frank, Thomas. *What's the matter with Kansas?: How conservatives won the heart of America.* Macmillan, 2007.
13 Feldstein, Martin. "Did wages reflect growth in productivity?." *Journal of Policy Modeling* 30.4 (2008): 591–594.
14 Marsh, 159.
15 162.

THE POLITICS OF HIGHER EDUCATION   11

16 Roland-Holst, David, Kenneth A. Reinert, and Clinton R. Shiells. "NAFTA liberalization and the role of nontariff barriers." *The North American Journal of Economics and Finance* 5.2 (1994): 137–168.

17 Stiglitz, Joseph. *The price of inequality.* Penguin UK, 2012.

18 Power, Mark, Carlo Bonifazi, and Kevin C. Desouza. "The ten outsourcing traps to avoid." *Journal of Business Strategy* 25.2 (2004): 37–42.

19 Marsh, 167.

20 167.

21 168.

22 169.

23 169–170.

24 MSN Money, "Why parents shouldn't pay for college." http://money.msn.com/family-money/why-parents-shouldnt-pay-for-college.

25 Ryan, Richard M., and Edward L. Deci. "Intrinsic and extrinsic motivations: Classic definitions and new directions." *Contemporary Educational Psychology* 25.1 (2000): 54–67: 2.

26 Bracher, Mark. *Social symptoms of identity needs: Why we have failed to solve our social problems, and what to do about it.* Karnac Books, 2009; 5.

27 Ibid., xiii.

28 Kezar, Adrianna J., and John Burkhardt. *Higher education for the public good: Emerging voices from a national movement.* Jossey-Bass Inc Pub, 2005.

29 Wilkinson, Richard G., and Kate Pickett. *The spirit level.* Tantor Media, Incorporated, 2011: 51–59.

30 Ibid.

31 Putnam, Robert D. "Bowling alone: America's declining social capital." *Journal of Democracy* 6 (1995): 68.

32 Clinton's speech can be found at: http://www.cnn.com/US/9601/budget/01-27/clinton_radio/.

2
COLLEGE AND THE MYTH OF THE GOOD JOB

In order to motivate people to go to college and to increase the public funding for higher education, many politicians and school officials have argued that on average, people with college degrees make much more money than people without degrees. This argument concerning the return on investment of higher education is based on a major misunderstanding of statistics, which involves confusing correlation with causation. In other words, we know that on average, people with college degrees earn more, but we do not know if having a degree causes higher income. For instance, it is entirely possible that many of the people who go to college and earn degrees would still have been wealthy if they had not gone to college. This is because wealthier people go to college at a much higher rate, and they also graduate at a much higher rate.[1] These wealthy individuals begin life with much more family wealth and better financial connections and networks, and in many ways, a college degree certifies the wealth with which these people start.[2]

Another major issue is the role played by averages. For example, if I am in a room of 100 people with an average wealth of $50,000, and Bill Gates walks into the room, the average wealth shoots up to several hundred million. In the case of figuring out the average income gains of people with college degrees, the average is inflated by the high earners who have completed college.[3] Furthermore, many of the people in the top 10% are doctors, lawyers, and managers who all were required to have college degrees, and in this case, completing college does pay

COLLEGE AND THE MYTH OF THE GOOD JOB 13

off, but only a small percentage of the population has the chance of ever entering into these professions.[4] Thus, from a purely economic perspective, a college degree may be very good for some people, but it is unclear how it helps most people in terms of lifetime earnings. One way of thinking about this is to see the high-end job market as a lottery system where you have to buy a ticket to have a chance of winning; some people start off with many tickets, but only a few people can win.

Degree Deflation

Another problem with basing the need for a college degree on the desire to earn more money is the fact that just because we produce more people with degrees does not mean that we will create more jobs that need these degrees.[5] In fact, some economists believe that we are driving down the value of each degree by overproducing the number of people competing for the same jobs with the same degrees. One result of this system is what is called a buyer's market for labor: since so many people want to get the same job, employers can increase the job requirements while reducing the compensation. A highly competitive job market, then, not only forces down wages, but it also allows some jobs to now require degrees that were not required before, and this is what we are seeing in the service sector, where many clerical and sales jobs are now requiring a college degree instead of a high school degree. In fact, according to the 2014 McKinsey report on the future of U.S. employment, "48 percent of employed US college graduates are in jobs that require less than a four-year college education (indeed, more than 15 percent of taxi drivers and firefighters have a college degree today; only 1 to 2 percent had one in 1970)."[6] Clearly, we are witnessing a growing rate of degree deflation where people with college degrees are now working at jobs that did not use to require more than a high school degree.

The Academic Lottery Economy

Universities should understand this type of buyer's market because they have themselves created one of the tightest labor

14   COLLEGE AND THE MYTH OF THE GOOD JOB

systems by overproducing doctoral degrees and then hiring back the same people to teach at low wages. If we look at recent trends in higher education employment, we find the following:

Full-Time Tenured and Tenure-Track Faculty

1976—353,681
2011—436,293
Increase—23%

Graduate Student Employees

1976—160,086
2011—358,743
Increase—123%

Full-Time Executives

1976—97,003
2011—233,368
Increase—141%

Full-Time Non-tenure Track Faculty

1976—80,883
2011—290,238
Increase—259%

Part-Time Faculty

1976—199,139
2011—768,071
Increase—286%[7]

Since virtually everyone working in these job categories has graduated from college, it should be clear that earning a college degree does not provide a clear path to a good job. In fact, according to these statistics, higher education is now dominated by a growing cadre of part-time and insecure workers, who have replaced full-time tenured faculty as the central academic position.[8] Meanwhile, the number of full-time, well-compensated

COLLEGE AND THE MYTH OF THE GOOD JOB   15

managers has continued to increase, and we shall see that these trends mirror employment practices throughout the economy.[9]

One of the reasons why the vast majority of people teaching in higher education are now low-wage, part-time workers without benefits is that universities continue to produce more people with academic PhDs, even though the schools know there are very few well-paying, full-time tenure-track faculty positions.[10] To make matters even worse, universities use graduate students, who are pursuing their degrees, as cheap labor while they are in school, and then they hire them back as cheap labor once they attain their degrees.[11] An artificial buyer's market is created then by increasing the supply of qualified people so that it outstrips the number of available positions and therefore drives down wages and benefits for everyone, which, in turn, leaves more money for the managers at the top.[12] Similar to the general economy, this system thrives on replacing full-time positions with part-time positions, and the result is that many more people are structurally underemployed.[13]

The STEM Degree Myth

An important myth that the employment practices of universities disprove is the idea that education and employment are directly related. In opposition to this myth, we shall see why good degrees do not produce good jobs, and in many cases, the opposite is actually the case. For example, many politicians, citizens, and school officials believe that we need to produce more students with STEM (Science, Technology, Engineering, and Math) degrees because this is where the jobs are in the present and the future. However, what may be going on is that employers are seeking to drive down the wages in these areas by creating a buyer's market through the overproduction of people with STEM degrees.

According to the article "The STEM Crisis Is a Myth," "there are more STEM workers than suitable jobs. One study found, for example, that wages for U.S. workers in computer and math fields have largely stagnated since 2000. Even as the Great Recession

16   COLLEGE AND THE MYTH OF THE GOOD JOB

slowly recedes, STEM workers at every stage of the career pipeline, from freshly minted grads to mid- and late-career Ph.D.s, still struggle to find employment as many companies, including Boeing, IBM, and Symantec, continue to lay off thousands of STEM workers."[14] In the face of this decrease in STEM-related job opportunities, we are reminded that "President Obama has called for government and industry to train 10,000 new U.S. engineers every year as well as 100,000 additional STEM teachers by 2020. And until those new recruits enter the workforce, tech companies like Facebook, IBM, and Microsoft are lobbying to boost the number of H-1B visas—temporary immigration permits for skilled workers—from 65,000 per year to as many as 180,000."[15] In other words, high-tech companies are pushing for increased access to high-skilled foreign workers in order to drive down labor costs and produce a more competitive labor market. Meanwhile, government officials are calling for a massive increase in funding to educate people for jobs that may not exist.

One of the major reasons why the government seems to have it wrong is the way STEM jobs are defined: "According to Commerce, 7.6 million individuals worked in STEM jobs in 2010, or about 5.5 percent of the U.S. workforce. That number includes professional and technical support occupations in the fields of computer science and mathematics, engineering, and life and physical sciences as well as management. The NSF [the National Science Foundation], by contrast, counts 12.4 million science and engineering jobs in the United States, including a number of areas that the Commerce Department excludes, such as health-care workers (4.3 million) and psychologists and social scientists (518,000)."[16] The first problem is then that the U.S. government itself has conflicting ways of defining who is working in a STEM job, and thus the National Science Foundation is able to call for more STEM funding by including in its ranks healthcare workers, psychologists, and social scientists. However, if we look at the more traditional understanding of STEM jobs, which is used by the Commerce Department, only 5.5% of all current U.S. jobs fall into this area.[17]

COLLEGE AND THE MYTH OF THE GOOD JOB 17

Not only is the STEM crisis being pushed by bad data and loose definitions, but it is also being fueled by a massive misunderstanding regarding the relationship between college degrees and future employment: "Of the 7.6 million STEM workers counted by the Commerce Department, only 3.3 million possess STEM degrees. Viewed another way, about 15 million U.S. residents hold at least a bachelor's degree in a STEM discipline, but three-fourths of them—11.4 million—work outside of STEM."[18] Thus, not only are there limited employment opportunities in the STEM areas, but most of the people with STEM degrees do not work in STEM jobs, and most of the people working in STEM jobs do not have STEM degrees. This loose connection between degrees and jobs means that there is not a pressing need to produce more people with STEM degrees, and non-STEM degree holders often end up being employed in STEM jobs. Moreover, on a more general scale, we see here how there is often a very loose connection between degrees, majors, and jobs: in contrast to popular myth, college majors do not predict very well the jobs at which students will end up working.

It is important to stress that the STEM labor market is very hard to predict and plan for because of the business and labor practices dominating these areas: "Highly competitive science- and technology-driven industries are volatile, where radical restructurings and boom-and-bust cycles have been the norm for decades. Many STEM jobs today are also targets for outsourcing or replacement by automation."[19] It turns out that the celebrated jobs in the STEM areas are very susceptible to downsizing, outsourcing, and boom-and-bust business cycles, and these economic trends make it difficult to predict where the jobs will be in the future and what type of college degrees students should pursue.

The unstable nature of STEM jobs is matched by the short-term thinking of many high-tech companies: "In engineering, for instance, your job is no longer linked to a company but to a funded project. Long-term employment with a single company has been replaced by a series of de facto temporary positions that

18   COLLEGE AND THE MYTH OF THE GOOD JOB

can quickly end when a project ends or the market shifts. To be sure, engineers in the 1950s were sometimes laid off during recessions, but they expected to be hired back when the economy picked up. That rarely happens today. And unlike in decades past, employers seldom offer generous education and training benefits to engineers to keep them current, so out-of-work engineers find they quickly become technologically obsolete."[20] Like so many other fields and professions, the older model of career employment has been replaced by a new system of just-in-time flexible labor, which, in turn, reduces the opportunity for job advancement since companies do not want to invest in workers who have no future with their corporations.[21] It is important to stress here that producing more people with college degrees will not change the employment practices of corporations; in fact, by focusing all of our attention on college as the pathway to the middle class, we fail to see the need to make major changes in how companies treat their employees.

Like the employment practices in higher education, wages in the STEM areas are being pushed down by an oversupply of future workers and an undersupply of new good jobs: "if you apply the Commerce Department's definition of STEM to the NSF's annual count of science and engineering bachelor's degrees, that means about 252,000 STEM graduates emerged in 2009. So even if all the STEM openings were entry-level positions and even if only new STEM bachelor's holders could compete for them, that still leaves 70,000 graduates unable to get a job in their chosen field. Of course, the pool of U.S. STEM workers is much bigger than that: It includes new STEM master's and Ph.D. graduates (in 2009, around 80,000 and 25,000, respectively), STEM associate degree graduates (about 40,000), H-1B visa holders (more than 50,000), other immigrants and visa holders with STEM degrees, technical certificate holders, and non-STEM degree recipients looking to find STEM-related work. And then there's the vast number of STEM degree holders who graduated in previous years or decades."[22] For people who work for a university or college, this story should be very familiar;

COLLEGE AND THE MYTH OF THE GOOD JOB   19

in the face of decreased job opportunities, colleges continue to flood the market with newly degreed workers, which then functions to drive down wages and create a class of underemployed and unemployed degree holders.

Why Politicians Believe in Education Myths

The creation of buyer's markets in higher education and the STEM fields contradict the following myths about higher education: (1) a college degree necessarily leads to economic mobility, (2) attaining a college degree results in attaining a good job, (3) we need more degrees to compete in the global economy, (4) we need more people to go to college, (5) college reduces poverty, (6) we need more STEM degrees, and (7) people with PhDs will get a good job. One way of countering these myths is to argue that in the current system, some people profit from earning a college degree, but when too many people earn the same degree, wages and employment are pushed down. Moreover, it is incredibly difficult to predict where the jobs will be in the future and which degrees will lead to good jobs.

However, since there is such a high payoff for some people who do complete their college degrees, the solution is not to tell people not to go to college; rather, we must even the playing field so that it is not only the wealthy who are able to increase their wealth by earning all of the tickets in the lottery economy. Also, public officials have to stop believing that education is the main solution to all our economic problems. Instead, we need to develop economic policies that help to expand the employment market for good jobs. For instance, the federal government needs to promote the ability of workers to organize for higher wages and job security, and it needs to avoid austerity measures that reduce good jobs in the public sector.[23] However, our government is not pursuing these types of policies because, in part, many politicians believe that all we need to do is to increase the number of people with college degrees.

Some public officials may want people to think that college is the answer to our economic problems because it is hard to deal with issues of globalization, de-unionization, taxation, deregulation, automation, discrimination, free trade, and employer greed. It is much easier to tell individuals that they can all succeed if they just work hard and go to college, but it is much harder to change our public policies to improve economic mobility. In short, the only way to increase the value of college degrees for everyone is to increase the number of good jobs, but what we are seeing is a downsizing and degrading of employment opportunities. Unlike Germany, Sweden, Norway, Finland, and Denmark, the United States has seen a major increase in wealth inequality coupled with a decrease in economic mobility.[24] Due to the lack of unionization and regulation and the focus on higher education as the solution to labor issues, the U.S. government can do very little to stop American businesses from replacing good jobs with part-time labor as companies search the world for the least expensive workers. Moreover, 30 years of tax cuts have reduced state and federal revenue, and the result has been a reduction of the social safety net and an increase in wealth inequality. Once again, producing more people with college degrees will not fix any of these problems.

The Mismatch Myth

Many businesses and politicians want people to believe that the reason why we have high rates of unemployment and underemployment is that there is a mismatch between jobs, education, and skills. According to this theory, higher education is the solution because it will provide workers with the knowledge they need to compete for new jobs. Although the mismatch argument is very seductive, the facts on the ground do not support the idea that there are millions of job openings that would be filled if people just had a better skills and education match. In reality, this theory is a convenient story that policy makers and businesses like to tell in order to remove themselves from any responsibility. In fact, the following statement by the Minneapolis Federal Reserve Bank president, Narayana Kocherlakota, reveals how the mismatch theory helps to replace economic policy

COLLEGE AND THE MYTH OF THE GOOD JOB 21

with a renewed called for individuals to get a better education: "What does this change in the relationship between job openings and unemployment connote? In a word, mismatch. Firms have jobs, but can't find appropriate workers. The workers want to work, but can't find appropriate jobs. There are many possible sources of mismatch—geography, skills, demography—and they are probably all at work. Whatever the source, though, it is hard to see how the Fed can do much to cure this problem. Monetary stimulus has provided conditions so that manufacturing plants want to hire new workers. But the Fed does not have a means to transform construction workers into manufacturing workers. Of course, the key question is: How much of the current unemployment rate is really due to mismatch, as opposed to conditions that the Fed can readily ameliorate? The answer seems to be a lot. Most of the existing unemployment represents mismatch that is not readily amenable to monetary policy."[25] Thus, as the Federal Reserve pumped trillions of dollars into banks and companies to stabilize the economy and keep interest rates low, this Fed banker did not believe that the government could do anything to help unemployment and underemployment because this economic problem was due to the mismatch between workers' skills and job opportunities.[26] Of course, we know that when he made this statement in 2010, there were many more qualified workers than job openings, but this fact does not matter because his perceptions were shaped by political myths concerning the role of education in the economy.

Lawrence Mishel, in his study "Education Is Not the Cure for High Unemployment or for Income Inequality," disproves the mismatch theory by documenting how during the Great Recession, workers with all levels of education in a wide range of employment areas lost their jobs.[27] In fact, it is absurd to think that from 2007 to 2010, millions of workers suddenly lost their skills and became victims of a mismatch between job opportunities and education. Although many politicians argue that due to technological changes in the workplace, workers no longer have the right skills, and so they need more education, Mishel shows

22   COLLEGE AND THE MYTH OF THE GOOD JOB

that education has very little to do with recent unemployment trends. What the promoters of the structural mismatch theory fail to mention is that the number of qualified people looking for each job increased dramatically after the Great Recession.[28] The problem, then, is not too little education or a lack of the right skills; the problem is the lack of job openings, and the result is a creation of a buyer's market for labor, where employers can require more education but pay their workers less.

A related myth to the mismatch theory is the idea that in the recovery following the Great Recession, people with college degrees did much better, and so education really did pay off. However, once again, the facts on the ground do not support this theory: "Workers with less education have higher unemployment rates at every point in the business cycle, but the unemployment rate has more than doubled for every education group over the downturn. Unemployment rose for each education group in the last year *except* the least-educated—those lacking a high school degree—a finding not very supportive of a recent twist against the least-educated workers."[29] Therefore, having a college degree did not prevent people from becoming unemployed, which would indicate that education does not directly determine employment possibilities. According to Mishel, "The biggest strike against the structural unemployment claim is that every education group has a similar share of its unemployment as long-term unemployed. Therefore, it seems that all workers once they are unemployed have a similar probability of being unemployed for at least 27 weeks regardless of their education level. That means that there is no particular education skew fueling the rise of long-term unemployment, just as we saw with overall unemployment in the previous table. If there has been some transformation of the workplace leaving millions of workers inadequate for the currently available jobs, as the structural unemployment claim would venture, then this transformation was definitely not based on a major educational upscaling of jobs, or at least that is what the unemployment data are telling us."[30] Since education level does not affect who ends up experiencing long-term unemployment, the supposed college degree bonus is not a major factor in determining the mismatch between jobs and skills. Moreover, as we know from the academic labor market, there is a prejudice against hiring unemployed and underemployed workers, and degree attainment does not seem to change this; as in the case of part-time faculty, the myth here is that if you have been unemployed or underemployed, there is something wrong with you and not the employers or the labor market.[31]

To reveal the problems with the now-dominant mismatch theory of structural unemployment, Mishel cites David Autor on the effects of the Great Recession on hiring practices: "Although the U.S. labor market will almost surely rebound from the Great Recession, this paper presents a somewhat disheartening picture of its longer-term evolution. Rising demand for highly educated workers, combined with lagging supply, is contributing to higher levels of earnings inequality. Demand for middle-skill jobs is declining, and consequently, workers that do not obtain postsecondary education face a contracting set of job opportunities."[32] Like many others, Autor believes that the employment payoff for a college degree increased after 2009 because of the loss of good middle-class jobs and the increase in low-wage employment. Autor continues by affirming that "an increased supply of college graduates should eventually help to drive down the college wage premium and limit the rise in inequality."[33] According to this theory, an increase in people with college degrees will decrease the value of workers with these degrees, which will in turn narrow the widening gap between high-wage and low-wage workers. However, in a buyer's labor market, some people will be sorted into high-wage jobs, while many more people will end up either unemployed or underemployed. Furthermore, this model of decreased income inequality is based on the idea that everyone will have their wages reduced, and in this process, the distance between people with and without degrees will also decrease.

As Mishel highlights, one of the major problems concerning the myth that a college degree leads to high lifetime earnings is the fact that economists do not distinguish between four-year

24   COLLEGE AND THE MYTH OF THE GOOD JOB

degrees and graduate and professional degrees: "For instance, in 2009 the unemployment rate among all college graduates was 4.6%, but those with at most a bachelor's degree had a rate of 5.2% and those with advanced degrees had a rate of 3.4%."[34] Even though people with advanced degrees have a much lower unemployment rate, these statistics do not allow us to see if someone is working at a job below their degree level. Moreover, statistics about earnings for college graduates or people with advanced degrees fail to take into account the growing inequality of compensation within groups of workers who have attained the same education level: "Most of the growth of wage inequality— the wage gap between a high-wage and low-wage worker—can be explained by increased wage gaps among workers with the same education (e.g., the inequality of wages among college graduates) than by wage gaps between workers of different educations (e.g., the college wage premium). That being the case, then even if greater college enrollment and completion could eliminate the wage gap between college graduates and other workers, much of wage inequality (and the greater extent of wage inequality now versus the past) would still remain, and wage inequality would continue to grow."[35] This finding renders problematic many of the claims politicians and school officials make about higher education: the production of more people with college degrees will not by itself decrease income inequality; rather, what we will continue to see is a growing disparity of wealth for people who have finished college.

Mishel's research also undermines several other myths concerning the relation between attaining a college degree and increasing one's wealth potential: "it is noteworthy that the jobs obtained by young college graduates in recent years pay less than the jobs obtained by those graduating five and 10 years earlier, both in terms of their wages and in the probability that employers provide health insurance or pension coverage."[36] As degree inflation pushes down the value of individual degrees, the previous college premium for earners has dissolved, and still many politicians and promoters of higher education do not want

COLLEGE AND THE MYTH OF THE GOOD JOB 25

to face this fact. Mishel concludes that "the rapid growth of the need for college graduates is not a juggernaut launched in the early 1980s that continues to this day: rather, the relative demand for college graduates has been slowing down in each decade since the 1980s and is now growing at a historically slow pace. It is this slow pace of the most recent period that might be the best clue to the future needs for college graduates."[37] Although it is hard to predict future employment needs, Mishel's research uses current data to show that in the present labor structure, there is not a growing need for more college graduates. In other words, much of the common understanding about higher education and employment opportunities is wrong.

Producing Underemployment

In "Unemployment: A Jobs Deficit or a Skills Deficit?," John Miller and Jeannettte Wicks-Lim argue that although political officials, like President Obama, believe that the future for jobs in America is in the high-tech industries that dominate in the media's coverage of business trends, actual labor data paint a very different picture: "President Obama's claim that new jobs are requiring higher and higher skill levels would tend to support the skills-gap thesis. His interpretation of job-market trends, however, misses the mark. The figure that Obama cited comes from the U.S. Department of Labor's employment projections for 2006 to 2016. Specifically, the DOL reports that among the 30 fastest growing occupations, 22 of them (75%) will typically require more than a high school degree. These occupations include network systems and data communications analysts, computer software engineers, and financial advisors. What he fails to say, however, is that these 22 occupations are projected to represent less than 3% of all U.S. jobs. What would seem more relevant to the 27 million unemployed and underemployed workers are the occupations with the largest growth. These are the occupations that will offer workers the greatest number of new job opportunities. Among the 30 occupations with the largest growth, 70%—21 out of 30—typically do not require more than a high

26   COLLEGE AND THE MYTH OF THE GOOD JOB

school degree. To become fully qualified for these jobs, workers will only need on-the-job training. The DOL projects that one-quarter of all jobs in 2016 will be in these 21 occupations, which include retail salespeople, food-preparation and food-service workers, and personal and home care aides."[38] It should be clear from these employment statistics that most new jobs will be in the low-wage sector; however, in the buyer's market, employers can now demand a college degree to perform a low-skill job at low wages. Meanwhile, the much-touted areas related to finance and computer engineering represent a small number of new job opportunities.

Perhaps the most disquieting aspect of our new labor economy is the number of employees who want to work more hours at their current jobs but have been hired at a lower rate, and so are considered to be underemployed. In 2014, the federal government estimated that 48% of recent college graduates were underemployed.[39] As Miller and Wicks-Lim argue, the persistence of underemployment flies in the face of the claim that workers just don't have the right skills or the proper education level: "Purveyors of the mismatch theory would have a hard time explaining how it is that underemployed workers who want full-time work do not possess the skills to do the jobs full-time that they are already doing, say, 20 hours a week."[40] Since so many people are now considered to be underemployed, it is difficult to see how increased education would improve their employment situation. In fact, in higher education, over two-thirds of the current faculty are part-time employees, and many of these professionals would like to work more, but they are just not given the opportunity to work full-time.

In the case of the broader economy, at the same time we are witnessing degree deflation, wage depression, and massive underemployment, corporations are sitting on a record level of cash, and so current labor practices cannot be blamed on the need to reduce costs for economic survival: "If businesses have barely resumed hiring, it has not been for lack of profits. By the middle of 2010, corporate profits (adjusted for inflation)

COLLEGE AND THE MYTH OF THE GOOD JOB 27

were about 60% above their low point at the end of 2008, well on their way back to the peak level of mid-2006. Also, in early 2010 non-financial firms were sitting on almost $2 trillion in cash. There was no lack of ability to invest and hire, but there was a lack of incentive to invest and hire, that is, a lack of an expectation that demand (sales) would rise. As is well known, small businesses have generally accounted for a disproportionately large share of job growth. Yet, since the onset of the Great Recession, small business owners have consistently identified poor sales as their single most important problem—and thus, presumably, what has prevented them from expanding employment."[41] After the Great Recession, many businesses reacted to the reduction in consumer demand by scaling back their operations and laying off workers or reducing their hours. However, once demand began to rise, many companies had grown to like their reduced use of full-time labor, and so, intentionally or unintentionally, they helped to create a buyer's market, which, in turn, drove down wages. Promoting a policy of more college graduates will not change this situation, and it may function to decrease the value of college degrees as the labor system replaces current workers without degrees with new, part-time workers with degrees.

The Middle-Class Myth

As President Obama has said on many occasions, a college degree is the path to the middle class; what Obama and others forget to add is that the middle class is disappearing, and so some college graduates are being sorted up, while most are being pushed down.[42] Moreover, as low-wage jobs increasingly require a college degree, people without these degrees are facing higher unemployment since they no longer are able to attain jobs that once only required a high school degree or less. The end result is that as the different earning potentials between the high- and low-income groups spread, the positions in the middle income level evaporate, even though most Americans believe that they are middle class.[43] According to *The New York Times*, "This up-credentialing is pushing the less educated even further down the food chain, and it helps explain why the unemployment rate for workers with no more than a high school diploma is more than twice that for workers with a bachelor's degree: 8.1 percent versus 3.7 percent."[44] Therefore, a college degree does help in the job competition, but most people are now competing for low-wage, low-skill jobs.

If we look at the rate of unemployment and underemployment for college graduates in 2012, we discover that over 50% fell into this category. This means that more than half of recent graduates did not have a job or the job they had did not match their degrees or training.[45] In a breakdown of what jobs these new graduates are doing, a *USA Today* study found the following: "they were more likely to be employed as waiters, waitresses, bartenders and food-service helpers than as engineers, physicists, chemists and mathematicians combined (100,000 versus 90,000). They were more likely working in office-related jobs such as receptionist or payroll clerk than in all computer professional jobs (163,000 versus 100,000). More also were employed as cashiers, retail clerks and customer representatives than engineers (125,000 versus 80,000)." The result, then, of degree inflation is a national pushing down of wages as people with college degrees are displacing people with high school degrees: "According to government projections released last month, only three of the 30 occupations with the largest projected number of job openings by 2020 will require a bachelor's degree or higher to fill the position—teachers, college professors and accountants. Most job openings are in professions such as retail sales, fast food and truck driving, jobs which aren't easily replaced by computers."[46] Even though many of the fastest growing jobs do not need to require college degrees, we have seen that they are making this requirement; meanwhile, colleges themselves are hiring most of their teachers off of the tenure track, and this means that they often do not have PhDs. The end result of these dual processes of degree deflation and de-professionalization is that middle-class jobs are turning into low-income positions.[47]

COLLEGE AND THE MYTH OF THE GOOD JOB 29

One reason why people do not know the true state of jobs in America is that politicians and school officials have bought into the myth that most future jobs will require a college degree. Although the economy could evolve in this direction, there is no proof that this will happen, and in fact, most evidence points in the exact opposite direction. The real story is that in a buyer's market, employers can require degrees that are not needed, and so the competition increases for a small number of jobs at the top and a large number of jobs at the bottom. Not only can employers push down wages in this type of system, but they can also require more from their workers.[48]

As degree inflation pushes down the wages of people with college degrees and displaces people who have not completed college, a relatively small number of people reap the benefits of productivity increases. For instance, if we look at the relation between median wages and productivity since 1940, we see that up to the early 1970s, these two economic trends increased together, but suddenly these two movements diverged, and now there is a huge separation between wages and economic productivity.[49] Although there are many explanations for this divergence, the main ones appear to be (1) globalization, (2) automation, (3) financialization, (4) deregulation, (5) de-unionization, (6) taxation, (7) immigration, and (8) women entering into the labor market. Interestingly, few of the factors appear to be directly connected to higher education. In fact, the earlier analysis does indicate that if higher ed has played a role in this process, it is by decreasing wages through degree inflation, underemployment, and the creation of a buyer's market for labor. Furthermore, during this period of the great separation between productivity and wages, we have also seen a tremendous increase in wealth inequality, and so we know that as workers have actually increased their economic productivity, their wages have not kept up, but high earners have gotten much more wealthy.

One part of this story is that the rich have found ways to keep an increasing share of the profits generated from increased productivity, but the other part is the way that wealthy people

30 COLLEGE AND THE MYTH OF THE GOOD JOB

have been able to magnify their wealth and political power.[50] Of course, a major reason for the growing income gap is the financialization of the economy, which allows wealthy people to invest their money in the stock market and other sectors that can provide a large payoff. Since non-wealthy people do not have the money to capitalize on financial markets, they have a much harder time increasing their wealth, and due to the Great Recession, many middle- and lower-income individuals have lost their savings and mortgage values, and so they are less able to invest.[51] Making matters worse is the way that higher education also tends to increase the distance between the wealthy few and the rest.

The Poor Get Poorer through Higher Education

Although a college degree no longer provides a clear path to a well-paying job, a college degree does improve one's odds at landing one of the dwindling number of high-skill, high-pay employment opportunities. However, in order to compete in this tight market, the importance of completing a four-year degree has gone up. Yet due to the role wealth plays in our higher ed system, the people who start off with a large wealth advantage can use higher education to increase their wealth, while low-income people can actually see their earnings potential decreased through higher education. In fact, we know that a wealthy student with poor grades has a much higher chance of completing a four-year degree than a poor student with high grades.[52] There are many reasons for this issue: (1) low-income students cannot afford to go to colleges with high graduation rates, (2) many elite universities admit students because of the wealth of their parents, (3) low-income students do not have parents who know what it takes to get into elite schools, and (4) many high school advisors in low-income areas do not help their students get into the best schools.[53] The end result of this system is that low-income students tend to go to low-funded community colleges that have very low graduation rates, while high-income students go to rich colleges with high graduation rates.

COLLEGE AND THE MYTH OF THE GOOD JOB   31

Of course, the biggest way that poverty affects who earns college degrees from elite institutions is through the funding of K-12 schools. Students who come from low-income neighborhoods tend to have low-performing schools with low graduation rates and few opportunities to take college preparation courses.[54] Many of these disparities are caused by the way we fund K-12 schools through local taxes and the effects poverty has on the ability of students to do well in their classes. As Diane Ravitch argues in *The Reign of Error*, since we think education is the solution to all of our social problems, we fail to see how poverty and related issues prevent low-income students from competing on a level playing field.[55] Not only do poor students tend to go to poor schools, but their lack of good health can also prevent them from attending school at a regular rate.

Since the inequalities in K-12 education affect who goes to college and who succeeds once they get into college, higher education cannot be seen as the solution to all of our social and economic problems. However, if we look at many political officials, we see that their understanding of the relation between economics and education is often based on a set of shared myths. For example, in his speech in August 2013 at SUNY Buffalo, President Obama made the following argument: "Now, there aren't many things that are more important to that idea of economic mobility—the idea that you can make it if you try—than a good education. All the students here know that. That's why you're here. That's why your families have made big sacrifices—because we understand that in the face of greater and greater global competition, in a knowledge-based economy, a great education is more important than ever."[56] It is clear that Obama believes in two myths: one is that the key to economic mobility is education, and the other is that the key to winning the global competition in the knowledge-based economy is higher education. As I have been discussing, both of these myths are very misleading. First, both K-12 education and higher education tend to reinforce wealth inequality because wealthy people tend to go to wealthy schools and poor people tend to go to poor schools;

32   COLLEGE AND THE MYTH OF THE GOOD JOB

meanwhile, the middle class is being reduced and sorted into the two extremes. Second, schools do not produce good jobs, and educational policy does not substitute for economic policy. Moreover, as the analysis of the STEM job market earlier shows, the production of degrees in certain high-earning fields actually works to drive down wages and increase underemployment and unemployment. Also, the creation of a buyer's labor market means that employers can require college degrees for low-wage, low-skill jobs, which, in turn, pushes people without college degrees into unemployment and underemployment.

In the same speech, Obama built on his argument by stressing the role played by college completion: "A higher education is the single best investment you can make in your future. And I'm proud of all the students who are making that investment. And that's not just me saying it. Look, right now, the unemployment rate for Americans with at least a college degree is about one-third lower than the national average. The incomes of folks who have at least a college degree are more than twice those of Americans without a high school diploma. So more than ever before, some form of higher education is the surest path into the middle class."[57] This argument sums up most of the myths I have been debunking in this chapter: higher education is the best investment an individual can make because it leads to higher earnings and a lower unemployment rate. If only this were true, our public policy would be clear; however, it is not true, or more accurately, it is highly misleading because it confuses correlation with causation and education with economics.

The goal here is not to single out Obama or the Democrats because politicians on the Right and the Left buy into the same set of myths regarding higher education. One reason for this bipartisan consensus is that public officials are almost all examples of people who have done well in the system, and thus they believe that the system works. Ultimately, the central myth about higher education that drives our national debate and policy development is the idea that college degrees are the key to individual economic advancement. One of the problems with this myth is that it turns a public issue into a private concern, and it therefore

COLLEGE AND THE MYTH OF THE GOOD JOB   33

undermines the public support for public higher education. By stressing that people who earn college degrees earn more money, public officials emphasize the private benefits of higher education and not the public benefits, like the need for a well-educated public to make informed decisions in our democracy.

In terms of economic benefits, one of the major ways that higher education does help our system is by keeping millions of young people out of unemployment and off of public assistance. Moreover, higher education helps to smooth the transition from dependency on parents to being an independent individual and employee, and it also offers a time period for new adults to discover what they would like to do in the future and what they value and believe in as both individuals and citizens. If we take into account what higher education does and does not do, we can begin to make better political decisions about how it should and should not be supported. In short, we should not pour more money into higher education if we think that its only value is to increase the potential earnings of specific students or if we think that it will help the United States compete in the global economy. However, we should increase the support for higher education if we believe that it is an important social institution, and students should not be excluded or included based solely on the wealth of their parents.

To help make a public argument for public higher education, we not only have to overcome the economic myths discussed earlier, but we also have to look at the role played by financial aid in determining who goes and who graduates from college. As we shall see in the next chapter, the issue of financial aid is also surrounded by a series of political myths that prevent us from making fair and rational decisions regarding higher education.

Notes

1 Cabrera, Alberto F., and Steven M. La Nasa. "On the path to college: Three critical tasks facing America's disadvantaged." *Research in Higher Education* 42.2 (2001): 119–149.

2 Davies, Scott, and Neil Guppy. "Fields of study, college selectivity, and student inequalities in higher education." *Social Forces* 75.4 (1997): 1417–1438.

34   COLLEGE AND THE MYTH OF THE GOOD JOB

3 Murphy, Kevin, and Finis Welch. "Wage premiums for college graduates recent growth and possible explanations." *Educational Researcher* 18.4 (1989): 17–26.

4 Elman, Cheryl, and M. O. Angela. "The race is to the swift: Socioeconomic origins, adult education, and wage attainment1." *American Journal of Sociology* 110.1 (2004): 123–160.

5 Kirp, David L. "The earth is flattening the globalization of higher education and its implications for equal opportunity." *Higher Education and Equality of Opportunity: Cross-National Perspectives* (2010): 11.

6 McKinsey & Company. (2013). *Voice of the graduate.* Philadelphia, PA: Author. Retrieved from http://mckinseyonsociety.com/downloads/reports/Education/UXC001%20Voice%20of%20the%20Graduate%20v7.pdf.

7 The Academe Blog. "In an era of increasing fiscal constraints, an inexplicable shift in hiring patterns in higher education." http://academeblog.org/2014/04/21/in-an-era-of-increasing-fiscal-constraints-an-inexplicable-shift-in-hiring-patterns-in-higher-education/#more-6749.

8 Clawson, Dan. "Tenure and the future of the university." *Science* 324.5931 (2009): 1147–1148.

9 Ginsberg, Benjamin. *The fall of the faculty.* Oxford University Press, 2011.

10 Budd, Mike. "Degrees of shame: Adjuncts and GAs organize." *Jump Cut: A Review of Contemporary Media, available at: www. ejumpcut. org/archive/jc44* (2001).

11 Lafer, Gordon. "Graduate student unions organizing in a changed academic economy." *Labor Studies Journal* 28.2 (2003): 25–43.

12 Bousquet, Marc. "The waste product of graduate education: Toward a dictatorship of the flexible." *Social Text* 20.1 (2002): 81–104.

13 Belous, Richard S. "Rise of the contingent work force: The key challenges and opportunities." *The Washington and Lee Law Review* 52 (1995): 863.

14 Charette, Robert N. "The STEM crisis is a myth." *IEEE Spectrum (Aug. 30, 2013) (online at spectrum.ieee.org/at-work/education/the-stem-crisis-is-a-myth)* (2013).

15 Ibid.

16 Ibid.

17 Ibid.

18 Ibid.

19 Ibid.

20 Ibid.

21 Monden, Yasuhiro. *Toyota production system: An integrated approach to just-in-time.* CRC Press, 2011.

22 Charette.

23 Baker, Dean. *The myth of expansionary fiscal austerity.* No. 2010–2023. Center for Economic and Policy Research (CEPR), 2010.

24 Blanden, Joe, Paul Gregg, and Stephen Machin. "Intergenerational mobility in Europe and North America." *Report supported by the Sutton Trust, Centre for Economic Performance, London School of Economics* (2005).

COLLEGE AND THE MYTH OF THE GOOD JOB 35

25 Reuss, Alejandro. "Why is unemployment still so high?" www.dollarsandsense.org/archives/2011/0211reuss.html.

26 Goodfriend, Marvin. "Central banking in the credit turmoil: An assessment of Federal Reserve practice." *Journal of Monetary Economics* 58.1 (2011): 1–12.

27 Mishel, Lawrence. "Education is not the cure for high unemployment or for income inequality." (2011). www.epi.org/publication/education_is_not_the_cure_for_high_unemployment_or_for_income_inequality/.

28 Ibid.

29 Ibid.

30 Ibid.

31 Bewley, Truman F. "A depressed labor market as explained by participants." *The American Economic Review* (1995): 250–254.

32 Mishel.

33 Ibid.

34 Ibid.

35 Ibid.

36 Ibid.

37 Ibid.

38 Miller, John, and Jeannette Wicks-Lim. "Unemployment: A jobs deficit or a skills deficit?" *Dollars and Sense,* January/February. www.dollarsandsense.org/archives/2011/0111millerwickslim.html.

39 Vedder, Richard, Christopher Denhart, and Jonathan Robe. "Why are recent college graduates underemployed? University enrollments and labor-market realities." *Center for College Affordability and Productivity (NJI)* (2013). http://centerforcollegeaffordability.org/research/studies/underemployment-of-college-graduates.

40 Miller and Wicks-Lim.

41 Ibid.

42 Sullivan, Teresa A., Elizabeth Warren, and Jay Lawrence Westbrook. *The fragile middle class: Americans in debt.* Yale University Press, 2000.

43 *USA Today.* "Half of new graduates are jobless or underemployed." http://usatoday30.usatoday.com/news/nation/story/2012-04-22/college-grads-jobless/54473426/1.

44 Rampell, Catherine. "It takes a BA to find a job as a file clerk." *The New York Times* 19 (2013): www.nytimes.com/2013/02/20/business/college-degree-required-by-increasing-number-of-companies.html?pagewanted=all&_r=0.

45 *USA Today.* http://usatoday30.usatoday.com/news/nation/story/2012-04-22/college-grads-jobless/54473426/.

46 Ibid.

47 Toren, Nina. "Deprofessionalization and its sources: A preliminary analysis." *Work and Occupations* 2.4 (1975): 323–337.

48 Jacobs, Jerry A., and Kathleen Green. "Who are the overworked Americans?." *Review of Social Economy* 56.4 (1998): 442–459.

49 Mishel.

50 Piketty, Thomas. *Capital in the twenty-first century*. Harvard University Press, 2014.

51 Grusky, David B., Bruce Western, and Christopher Wimer, eds. *The great recession*. Russell Sage Foundation, 2011.

52 Mettler, Suzanne. *Degrees of inequality: How the politics of higher education sabotaged the American dream*. 2014: 26.

53 Keller, George. "The new demographics of higher education." *The Review of Higher Education* 24.3 (2001): 219–235.

54 Greene, Jay P., and Greg Forster. *Public high school graduation and college readiness rates in the United States*. Vol. 3. New York, NY: Center for Civic Innovation at the Manhattan Institute, 2003.

55 Ravitch, Diane. *Reign of error: The hoax of the privatization movement and the danger to America's public schools*. Random House LLC, 2013.

56 "Remarks by the president on college affordability—Buffalo, NY": www.whitehouse.gov/the-press-office/2013/08/22/remarks-president-college-affordability-buffalo-ny.

57 Ibid.

3

WHY HIGHER EDUCATION REDUCES SOCIAL MOBILITY?

Most Americans still believe in the myth that higher education promotes social mobility and allows people to move up the economic ladder. However, as I argued in the last chapter, low-income students tend to go to low-funded community colleges with low graduation rates, while high-income students tend to go to wealthy universities with high graduation rates. In fact, we know that in 2011, 70% of adults in the top income quartile attained four-year degrees, while only 10% in the bottom quartile have attained the same level of education.[1] If we compare this same statistic to 1970, we discover that 40% in the top group had four-year degrees and 6% in the bottom quartile had these degrees.[2] In other terms, the wealthy are becoming much more educated, while the poor have made only small gains. It is important to stress that during the last four decades, schools, states, and the federal government have spent trillions of dollars to use financial aid and tax breaks to make higher education more affordable to low- and moderate-income students, but the end result of this policy is that the total cost of attendance continues to go up as class stratification increases.[3] One of the main reasons for this lack of social mobility is that our current systems of financial aid are often counter-productive. Although financial aid does assist many people, it often does not help the students who need the most help, and it also aids people who need no help. Moreover, there are so many competing forms of financial aid that most citizens and public officials do not understand how the aid system works.

Poor Students with Cadillacs

Perhaps the biggest problem with the current understanding of college financial aid is that people do not know for what it does and does not pay. This lack of knowledge was evident in a 2014 hearing organized by the U.S. Senate Committee on Health, Education, Labor, and Pensions, which was discussing financial aid and the reauthorization of the Higher Education Act.[4] During his opening statement, the ranking Republican member, Lamar Alexander, set the stage by arguing that since the average cost for community college was about $3,000 and students receive over $4,000 in aid, some of the money must be going to other things. In fact, Alexander's own press release entitled "College More Affordable than Most Students Think" argued that "The average community college student in America is receiving about $1,500 more in grants and scholarships than it costs in tuition and fees."[5] The problem with Alexander's argument is that he fails to take into account the total cost of education (tuition, fees, room, board, books, and living expenses), and so he could pretend that there is no reason for students to borrow, and that if they are borrowing, it is for personal pleasure.

Driving this public official's misunderstanding are the common myths that college tuition is driving student debt and that financial aid covers the total cost of attendance for low-income students. Both of these statements are false, and they shape our ineffective aid policies. In reality, tuition only accounts for about a third of the total cost of attending colleges and universities, but politicians and school officials only talk about tuition because they do not want to think about who should pay for books, living expenses, room, and board. From a conservative perspective, college should not cost so much, and if it costs a lot, it is because schools are driving up the cost of tuition.[6] Moreover, from this view, since state, federal, and institutional grants cover the tuition of most low-income students, there is no need to increase the public funding for higher education, and if students do go into debt, it is because they are spending their aid on noneducational things like cars and iPhones.[7]

HIGHER ED AND SOCIAL MOBILITY 39

We see this logic in full effect when Alexander stated in the senate hearing that "An Inspector General's report from the U.S. Department of Education warns that some students borrow excessively for personal expenses not related to their education." What Alexander did not add is that it is clear that students need a place to live, and that they have to buy books for their classes, and so these non-educational expenses are actually the main cause for student debt. In fact, in 2013, the U.S. Department of Education reported that the total annual cost of attendance for a full-time community college student was $13,237, so if students received on average $4,500 in grant funding, they were still on the hook for close to $9,000 per year.[8]

Apparently, not only do Republicans like Lamar Alexander fail to understand the difference between the cost of tuition and the total cost of attendance, but also Democrats like James W. Runcie, Obama's Chief Operating Officer of Federal Student Aid of the Department of Education, do not seem to comprehend the reasons students borrow money to go to college. In response to Alexander's question about why students are taking out more money than they need, Runcie simply stated that this was a concern, and the department was looking into possible cases of fraud or abuse. We thus have a bipartisan consensus to buy into the myth that financial aid is only for tuition, and that students go into debt because they spend their aid on unnecessary non-educational expenses.

How the Private Became Public

As Suzanne Mettler discusses in her book *Degrees of Inequality*, one of the main reasons that our financial aid system is not working is that the aid for low-income students now only covers a small part of their total expenses.[9] In fact, during the 1970s, Pell Grants paid for 80% of a recipient's tuition, room, board, and expenses, while in 2012–2013, it only covered 31%.[10] During the same period, as Mettler points out, the government shifted some of its aid to tax breaks that mostly went to the wealthy.[11] The end result is that lower-income students have to go into massive debt to stay in school, and so many drop out or take extra years to graduate, which drives up the cost of each degree. Meanwhile, the public is subsidizing wealthy students through tax breaks that reduce the state and federal funds that could have been used to support higher education.[12] The end result is that well-intentioned financial aid plans often end up decreasing class mobility and increasing economic inequality.

Mettler also stresses that the government is now subsidizing for-profit higher education, and many of these institutions receive 90% of their funding through grants and student loans.[13] Even though these schools have very low graduation rates, sometimes below 10%, they continue to receive 25% of all federal financial aid ($32 billion in 2012) as they take in huge profits.[14] Like the subprime loan market for low-income families, these schools prey on poor people who are convinced that the path to the middle class is paved with student loans and higher education.[15] In fact, some progressive politicians have supported the for-profit college industry because they believed that this is the only segment that is taking care of low-income minority students who have been pushed out of public and private colleges and universities.[16] This liberal policy is similar to the idea that low-income families should be given subprime mortgages that they cannot afford.[17]

The promotion of for-profit corporate welfare has been a mostly bipartisan affair and supports many of the myths that circulate around financial aid. First, it turns out that a lot of the federal aid for higher education goes to for-profit and private colleges and universities.[18] This means that the private universities are not actually private. Moreover, as private citizens pay for more of the cost of attending public institutions, public colleges and universities are no longer publicly funded.[19] In this upside-down system, federal and state governments are using public funds for private schools as they reduce their support for public institutions. A side effect of this structure is that many wealthy private schools are receiving public aid, while public universities and colleges, which educate over 73% of the students, are forcing students to take out massive loans to pay for the gap between their financial aid and the total cost of attendance.[20]

Making matters worse is the fact that since the federal government took over most of the college loan business, the government has been making huge profits off of these students. The Congressional Budget Office claims that starting in 2013, the federal loan system will turn a $127 billion profit over a ten-year period.[21] If we step back and look at what has happened, we discover that after the financial meltdown of 2008, states cut their funding for higher education, and public universities and colleges responded by raising tuition. In response to the increase in the cost of attendance, students and parents took out a record level of student loans, and now the federal government is profiting off of this debt. Furthermore, the new student loan program was passed as part of the Affordable Care Act, and the legislation stipulates that any profits made from the loan program will go into the general fund and not higher education.[22]

Generating Poverty through Aid

It is now common knowledge that student loan debt has surpassed $1 trillion, but what most people do not know is that this type of debt has profound side effects.[23] One problem is that many students cannot afford to pay back their loans, and so the amount of money they owe increases dramatically due to penalties for delayed payment and default.[24] Making matters worse, it has been reported that many businesses now check the credit scores of prospective employees, and so when students fail to make a loan payment, they hurt their chance at getting a job.[25] Also, unlike other forms of debt, student loans cannot be reduced or removed through bankruptcy, and the federal government has the ability to garnish paychecks, tax returns, social security checks, and even disability checks.[26] If this was not bad enough, the federal government hires private debt collectors who have a financial incentive for students to default on their loans.[27]

42 HIGHER ED AND SOCIAL MOBILITY

One reason why the federal government spends several billion dollars each year on debt collectors is that these outside agencies receive bonuses for their aggressive handling of student debt.[28] In this system, outside agencies are given an incentive to harass students and force them to hand over all of their money to the collectors. Furthermore, since these private agencies increase their earnings if they collect more from students, they do not pursue other forms of reconciliation, like writing down the principal or extending the payments. In fact, borrowers in default are subject to the government's extraordinary collection powers that last a lifetime: "The collection agencies hold the keys to the borrower's future because the government hires collection agencies not only to collect, but also to act as the front line 'dispute resolution' entities for financially distressed borrowers."[29] In other words, the private collectors act as judge and jury, and they use the power of the national government to garnish wages and public benefits. This situation has gotten so bad that many people have had their social security checks garnished in order to pay back decades-old student loans.[30] As a society, we have created a system of indentured student servitude as our tax dollars are used to pay profit-seeking loan collectors to further abuse former students.[31] Making matters worse, when people are late on their loan payments, they often are subjected to huge penalties that make it even harder for them to pay off their debt, which transforms them into prime targets for aggressive for-profit debt collectors and exploitive private debt refinancers.

The New York Federal Reserve has reported that this massive student debt level may have a strong negative effect on the economy because these recent graduates are paying so much on their loans that they cannot afford to buy cars or homes, or start families.[32] Higher education, then, instead of being an engine of economic mobility and growth, has turned into a vehicle for economic stagnation and unemployment, and one of the main reasons for this reversal is our system of financial aid. Not only has the aid failed to keep up with rising costs and increased enrollments, but more of it now goes to wealthy families.[33]

From Need to Merit

Another major shift in financial aid has been the move from need-based aid to merit-based aid.[34] Since most people believe in the myth that financial aid is only for poor people, they do not understand that schools have turned to merit aid in order to compete for the "best" students with the highest SAT scores.[35] In this system, public and private colleges and universities often try to increase their rankings in *US News and World Report* by enrolling students with high SAT scores; however, we know that SAT scores are highly correlated with the wealth of the parents, and so the pursuit of high rankings results in giving an advantage to students coming from high-income families.[36] This advantage is enhanced because these schools increasingly base aid on merit, which is often based on SAT scores. The end result is that wealthy students have an advantage in getting into schools and also receiving aid from schools.

This use of merit aid also affects the difference between the sticker price for college and what people actually pay. In a similar fashion to an airplane ticket, most people are paying a different price to purchase the same good, and while much of the tuition reduction goes to low-income students, a lot of it also goes to the wealthy students who would be able to attend without any aid. This generation of inequality is fueled by the fact that schools inflate their tuition for everyone in order to give merit aid to wealthy students and need-based aid to low-income students.[37] Since most of the aid is funneled to the wealthy and the poor, the people in the middle who do not qualify for need-based aid end up paying for the cost of tuition inflation due to aid policies. Many economists also believe that due to the availability of student loans and state and federal aid, some schools have an incentive to raise their tuition in order to make sure their students receive the maximum level of external aid.[38] This availability of aid, tuition tax breaks, and loans not only allows schools to inflate the cost of attendance, but it also helps states to decrease their direct support for higher education. Mettler

44 HIGHER ED AND SOCIAL MOBILITY

concludes that higher education and financial aid have not helped to level the playing field; rather, they have helped to increase income and educational inequality. This finding surely flies in the face of the popular myths about higher education and aid.

The Work-Study Myth

Many people believe that wealthy students graduate college at a higher rate because they do better at high school; however, Mettler shows that the low-income high school graduation rate is not that much lower than the high-income high school graduate rate, and 75% of all high school graduates go directly to college.[39] The major problem is that a very low percentage of low-income students gain four-year degrees. While 97% of the students from high-income families who attend four-year institutions attain their degrees by age twenty-four, only 23% of low-income students graduate by age twenty-four.[40] The issue therefore is not that too few low-income students enroll in college: the problem is that not enough of the students graduate, and one of the major reasons is that they cannot afford to stay in school. Not only do low-income students have to take on huge debt to pay for college, but also many are forced to work multiple jobs while in school. Once again, financial aid plays a role in this process because the federal government subsidizes work-study jobs, and colleges profit from paying low wages to their student workers. Furthermore, as low-income students spend many hours working to pay for their education, wealthier students who do not have to work have more time to study and pursue extra-curricular activities.[41]

In his book *How the University Works*, Marc Bousquet has documented how undergraduate students are not only working increased hours through campus jobs, but they have also now become a source for employment exploitation by local businesses.[42] Since many low-income students have to work to pay for the gap between their financial aid and the total cost of attending college, they are vulnerable to abusive employment practices, and the more these students work outside of the school, the longer it takes them to graduate—if they graduate at all.

In the case of graduate education, this system is even more pernicious because students often have to teach or do research as part of their financial aid, but because they spend so much time on these activities, many do not have time to finish their degrees.[43] Once again, wealthy students have a major advantage here because they often can rely on family support to complete their degrees, while low- and middle-income students have to work and go into massive debt in order to attain a degree that may only lead to a part-time job at the same or a different university. In fact, graduate students have the highest level of student loan debt and defaults.[44]

The solution to these problems is to make sure that financial concerns do not determine who goes or completes college, but our current system of financial aid is centered on a series of counter-productive myths. Since most politicians and citizens believe that higher education is the key to economic mobility, and financial aid levels the playing field, they do not see how our current system actually increases wealth inequality. What is so interesting is that while people have rejected the idea of using vouchers for K-12 education, college financial aid is a voucher system.[45] In this structure, individuals are given aid packages that they can use to attend the institutions of their choice, and many of these schools are not public colleges or universities.

Tax Welfare for the Wealthy

The federal government and many individual states have also turned to tax breaks for higher education because it is easier to pass a tax cut than to find support for additional funding. However, the major problem with this approach is that since most low-income families pay little if any federal or state income taxes, they are not eligible to take advantage of higher education tax deductions. Meanwhile, many wealthy people have turned to College 529 Savings Plans to shelter investment income from taxation. For instance, in 2013, there was over $200 billion in

46   HIGHER ED AND SOCIAL MOBILITY

these accounts, and most of the money was held by people making over $180,000.[46] The reason why this program is so attractive to the wealthy is that if you invest money and make a large return, you do not have to pay any taxes on the gains if you use it for higher education.

Like so many other financial aid policies, college savings plans started off with good intentions, but they were quickly gamed by the wealthy, and we see a similar issue with state tax breaks for tuition and educational expenses; only the wealthy with expensive accountants know how to work the system and get the most out of the tax code.[47] Using tax breaks to fund higher education thus represents another significant advantage that the wealthy gain from higher education, which, in turn, drives up wealth inequality. It should be pointed out that this manipulation of the tax code has been a bipartisan affair and feeds off of the myth that financial aid for college is inherently good.

Ripping Off Vets

In 2012, the United States also spent over $12 billion on financial aid for the military, and some of this money went to for-profit schools, which left many veterans with huge debts and no degrees.[48] In fact, several wealthy for-profit schools successfully lobbied Congress in 2006 to drop the requirement that at least 50% of their classes had to be on campus for students to qualify for student aid.[49] Since many active military taking courses would benefit from this change, it seemed like a good idea, but the result was a major increase in online for-profit schools that only dedicate a low proportion of their funds to instructional activities. It has been revealed that for-profit schools often spend most of their money on advertising, administration, recruitment, and executive compensation, and virtually all of their faculty are part-time without the possibility of tenure or any of the benefits traditionally associated with professorial positions.[50] Several of these schools are parts of national chains that have gone public and now trade shares on the stock exchange, and even though they get almost all of their funding from the federal government, they bring in huge profits every year.[51] Since it is often low-income students and former and present military personnel who attend these schools, we find here another example of public financial aid used to increase income inequality and decrease social mobility.[52]

The Myth of Need-Blind Admissions

So far, we have seen that the myths circling around financial aid mislead students, politicians, and parents about the effectiveness of the programs that are supposed to make college affordable and accessible to all. Due to the gap between financial aid and the actual total cost of attendance, many low- and moderate-income students are forced to take out huge loans and work long hours in school, and still, at the end of this expensive journey, the majority have not earned a degree. We have also seen that much of our public support for higher education is actually going to private institutions, and since aid is being switched from need to merit, we see an increase in support for wealthy students at the expense of low- and middle-income students. This redistribution of public funds from the bottom to the top is coupled with admissions policies that favor the wealthy over the poor.

Although many schools claim that they are need blind, which means they do not take into account a student's ability to pay when they decide to accept or reject that student, we now know that this is not the case.[53] It turns out that many need-blind schools do look at the financial status of students before they make admissions decisions. In fact, if a student simply checks off the box on the FASFA form that he or she will be applying for aid, the chance of that student being accepted is decreased, and since many schools rely on tuition to function, they have a strong incentive to accept students who can pay all or most of the cost of attendance.

Even if a student does gain admissions to a college or university and is offered financial aid, the student is not out of the dark because many schools offer students more aid the first year than the following years in order to get the students in the door. In a

48 HIGHER ED AND SOCIAL MOBILITY

process known as frontloading, financial aid offices make large offers to freshman admits, only to later reduce the aid once they become sophomores.[54] Moreover, many aid packages come with requirements that the student may not be able to fulfill, and then the student has to decide whether to stay in school and finish the process even though the financial aid has disappeared. In the case of graduate students, the situation is even worse because each year they have to compete for scholarships, research positions, and teaching assistantships, and since they often take ten years to complete their doctoral degrees, there is a good chance that their aid will be decreased or eliminated.

Due to this inconsistent and inadequate financial aid system, it should be no surprise that since 1990, more students are going to college, but only the students coming from wealthy families are increasing their graduation rates.[55] A major reason why rich students are completing college at a much higher rate is that the net cost of attendance only takes up a small percentage of their annual income, while for low- and moderate-income students, the net cost is sometimes higher than 50% of the family's income. For example, if a low-income student, whose family earns $21,000 per year, goes to a four-year public university, the cost will equal 59% of the family's income. In the case of a wealthy student, with a family income of $142,000, the net cost will only be $16,000, and this is after financial aid is taken into consideration.[56] The divergence between what poor and wealthy families have to pay to go to college is in part driven by the simultaneous decrease in family incomes for most Americans and the constant rise in the total cost of college attendance. Since financial aid programs have not kept up with this growing inequality, students and their families have turned to loans to pay for college.[57]

One of the effects of the growing wealth inequality in America is that more people are going to college in order to get ahead, but the financial aid systems cannot keep up with the growing need. Therefore, although Pell Grants have gone up, they have not kept up with the rise in costs and the decrease in median

HIGHER ED AND SOCIAL MOBILITY 49

family wealth. Once again, we see how we cannot separate higher education policy from broader economic issues, and the political focus on aid and college completion blinds us from seeing how we need to develop better policies concerning employment, income, and taxation. For example, a growing number of students are now low-income single mothers, but when these students receive financial aid, they end up losing most of their benefits like food stamps and housing subsidies.[58]

Separate and Unequal

As financial aid is working to make many low-income students poorer, higher education institutions are becoming increasingly unequal in terms of their funding and racial, economic, and ethnic makeup. In looking at what colleges low- and high-income students tend to attend, we find that poorer students are being segregated into poorly funded community colleges that are often populated by underrepresented minority students, while wealthy students tend to go to wealthy private schools catering to white, Asian, and international students. According to Richard Kahlenberg's "Magnifying Social Inequality": "Low-income and minority students are concentrated in community colleges, which spent an average of $12,957 per full-time-equivalent student in 2009, while higher-income and white students are disproportionately educated at private four-year research institutions, which spent an average of $66,744 per student."[59] Just as underrepresented minority and low-income students attend the K-12 schools with the lowest funding per student, the same occurs in the case of higher education. The result is that the students who often need the most help and attention are attending schools that cannot afford to provide support. Moreover, Kahlenberg adds that wealthy students have a huge advantage through the admissions' process: "legacy preferences for the children of alumni increase one's chance of admissions by 45 percentage points, aiding an already highly privileged group." This is one way that the rich get richer as the poor get poorer: the wealthy have a much higher chance of getting into a highly

50 HIGHER ED AND SOCIAL MOBILITY

funded college, while low-income students tend to go to schools with low funding and low graduation rates. One result of this inequality is the growing divergence of graduation rates between the two income groups: "A University of Michigan study found that the disparity in college completion rates between students from wealthy families and poor ones has grown by 50 percent since the 1980s."[60] Therefore, instead of higher education being a vehicle for social mobility, it has become a great magnifier of wealth inequality.

Although we are currently experiencing a devaluing of college degrees and a tightening of labor markets, people who attend selective colleges and universities have a great advantage in pursuing advanced degrees and high-income jobs. In fact, just as the value of a high school degree in the job market has decreased, the bachelor degree is also losing its value, and so the real payoff has moved up to advanced degrees. Looking at recent enrollment data for higher education, we see how an increasing number of people are going to graduate school in order to compete in the competitive job market. In fact, from 2000 to 2009, the number of males enrolled in graduate school went up 36%, while the number of females went up 63%.[61] Since we know that the unemployment rate for people with advanced degrees is much lower than the rate for people with bachelor degrees, this large increase in graduate school enrollment signals another way that higher education can result in increased income inequality.

A Fairer Model for Financial Aid

A more coherent financial aid policy would recognize the need to eliminate public funding for private and for-profit colleges in order to shift funds to the public schools that educate over 70% of the students. This process should also entail an elimination of tax breaks for higher ed coupled with a shift of aid from individual students to the public institutions they attend. In turn, to make sure that aid does not result in tuition increases, participating schools need to be prohibited from increasing tuition and

HIGHER ED AND SOCIAL MOBILITY

other costs higher than the rate of inflation, and states must be required to maintain or increase their support for public higher education. As I argued in my book, *Why Public Higher Education Should Be Free*, we could make all public higher education free to the students by just using current resources in a fairer and more efficient manner.[62] Part of this change would require the elimination of the current student loan system and a discontinuation of the process where schools raise their tuition to offset the cost of their own financial aid packages.

Although some think that this plan would increase dramatically the number of students attending public colleges and universities and thus drive up the cost of public higher education and decrease the value of degrees, the goal is to make sure that personal finances are not the reason why people do not enroll or graduate. If we remove the cost to the individual, more people would move through the system at a faster rate, which would open up new spaces for additional enrollments. However, since I have shown that education policy does not replace employment policy, we still need to couple a fairer higher education system with a better employment structure. In other words, we have to fix the way we finance higher education at the same time we restructure the job market.

Of course, one reason why it is hard to even imagine changing any aspect of our economy is that rich individuals and corporations have used their wealth to capture the government, and so higher education and economic policies tend to heighten wealth inequality and decrease social mobility. In terms of higher education, our guiding principle should be that at the very least, it should do no harm. Moreover, the counter-productive myths that dominate financial aid for higher education have to be linked to the question of why tuition continues to increase and why students seem to be paying more and getting less.

Notes

1 Mettler, Suzanne. *Degrees of inequality: How the politics of higher education sabotaged the American dream*. Basic Books, 2014.
2 Ibid.

3 For the total annual cost of state and federal support for higher education, see http://trends.collegeboard.org/sites/default/files/student-aid-2013-full-report.pdf.

4 The higher education hearing can be accessed at: www.help.senate.gov/hearings/hearing/?id=be24605b-5056-a032-5264-da1396baca15.

5 Alexander's press release is at: www.help.senate.gov/newsroom/press/release/?id=51458a84-452b-404e-8cc2-6c5840c67004&groups=Ranking.

6 Gillen, Andrew. "Introducing Bennett Hypothesis 2.0." *Center for College Affordability and Productivity (NJ1)* (2012).

7 Carr, Neil. "Poverty, debt, and conspicuous consumption: University students' tourism experiences." *Tourism Management* 26.5 (2005): 797–806.

8 National statistics on cost of attendance and aid can be found at: http://nces.ed.gov/programs/digest/d13/tables/dt13_330.40.asp.

9 Mettler, Suzanne. *Degrees of inequality: How the politics of higher education sabotaged the American dream.* 2014: 9–11.

10 Ibid.

11 Ibid.

12 Burd, Stephen, et al. *"Rebalancing resources and incentives in federal student aid." New America Foundation* (2013).

13 Mettler, 3.

14 Ibid.

15 Lynch, Mamie, Jennifer Engle, and José L. Cruz. *"Subprime opportunity: The unfulfilled promise of for-profit colleges and universities." Education Trust* (2010).

16 Mettler, 3.

17 Warren, Elizabeth. "Economics of race: When making it to the middle is not enough." *The Washington and Lee Law Review* 61 (2004): 1777.

18 For statistics on what types of students and institutions receive federal aid, see http://nces.ed.gov/programs/digest/d13/tables/dt13_331.90.asp.

19 Singell Jr, Larry D., and Joe A. Stone. "For whom the Pell tolls: The response of university tuition to federal grants-in-aid." *Economics of Education Review* 26.3 (2007): 285–295.

20 Mettler, 11.

21 "CBO's April 2014 baseline projections for the student loan program": www.cbo.gov/sites/default/files/cbofiles/attachments/44198-2014-04-StudentLoan.pdf.

22 C-SPAN. "Federal Student Loan Program": www.c-span.org/video/?c4494563/sen-warren-runcie.

23 Obama, President Barack. "State of the union address." (2010).

24 Gladieux, Lawrence, and Laura Perna. "Borrowers who drop out: A neglected aspect of the college student loan trend. National Center Report# 05-2." *National Center for Public Policy and Higher Education* (2005).

25 Cude, Brenda, et al. "College students and financial literacy: What they know and what we need to learn." *Proceedings of the Eastern Family Economics and Resource Management Association* (2006): 102–109.

HIGHER ED AND SOCIAL MOBILITY 53

26 Collinge, Alan. *The student loan scam: The most oppressive debt in US history, and how we can fight back.* Beacon Press, 2009.

27 Stiglitz, Joseph E. "Student debt and the crushing of the American dream." *The New York Times* (2013).

28 Loonin, Deanne, and Jillian McLaughlin. "Borrowers on hold: Student loan collection agency complaint systems need massive improvement." *National Consumer Law Center (May 2012)* (2012): 15.

29 Ibid.

30 Lewin, Tamar. "Burden of college loans on graduates grows." *New York Times* (2011).

31 Williams, Jeffrey J. "Student debt and the spirit of indenture." *Dissent* 55.4 (2008): 73–78.

32 New York Federal Reserve. "Quarterly report on household debt and credit": www.newyorkfed.org/research/national_economy/household credit/DistrictReport_Q42012.pdf.

33 The Hechinger Report. "College, federal financial aid increasingly benefits the rich": http://hechingerreport.org/content/college-federal-financial-aid-increasingly-benefits-rich_15001/.

34 College Board. "Trends in student aid, 2013." *Trends in Higher Education Series*, 2013b; https://trends.collegeboard.org/sites/default/files/student-aid-2013-full-report-140108.pdf.

35 Willsey, Marie. "How do SAT scores affect financial aid?": http://money.howstuffworks.com/personal-finance/college-planning/financial-aid/sat-score-affect-financial-aid.htm.

36 Goldfarb, Zachary. *The Washington Post Blog.* "These four charts show how the SAT favors rich, educated families": www.washingtonpost.com/blogs/wonkblog/wp/2014/03/05/these-four-charts-show-how-the-sat-favors-the-rich-educated-families/.

37 *USA Today.* "Propublica: Colleges cater financial aid to wealthy": www.usatoday.com/story/news/nation/2013/09/12/propublica-colleges-financial-aid-low-income-access/2806509/.

38 Singell Jr, Larry D., and Joe A. Stone. "For whom the Pell tolls: The response of university tuition to federal grants-in-aid." *Economics of Education Review* 26.3 (2007): 285–295.

39 Mettler, 25.

40 Ibid.

41 Walpole, MaryBeth. "Socioeconomic status and college: How SES affects college experiences and outcomes." *The Review of Higher Education* 27.1 (2003): 45–73.

42 Bousquet, Marc, and Cary Nelson. *How the university works: Higher education and the low-wage nation.* NYU Press, 2008.

43 Mettler, 27.

44 Delisle, Jason. "The graduate student debt review: The state of graduate student borrowing." (2014).

45 Ravitch, Diane. *The death and life of the great American school system: How testing and choice are undermining education.* Basic Books, 2011.

46 Burd, Stephen. "Moving on up: How tuition tax breaks increasingly favor the upper-middle class." *Education Sector* (2012).

47 Ibid.

48 The Hill. "Taxpayer dollars funding deceptive practices of for-profit colleges": http://thehill.com/blogs/congress-blog/education/202610-taxpayer-dollars-funding-deceptive-practices-of-for-profit.

49 Mettler, 106.

50 Kirkham, Chris. "For-profit colleges spend much less on educating students than public universities,‖." *Huffington Post* (2011).

51 Mettler, 106.

52 www.motherjones.com/politics/2014/01/for-profit-college-student-debt.

53 www.huffingtonpost.com/the-brown-daily-herald/the-illusion-of-needblind_b_2854705.html.

54 Linsenmeier, David M., Harvey S. Rosen, and Cecilia Elena Rouse. *Financial aid packages and college enrollment decisions: An econometric case study.* No. w9228. National Bureau of Economic Research, 2002.

55 Goldrick-Rab, Sara, and Nancy Kendall. "Redefining college affordability: Securing America's future with a free two year college option": www.luminafoundation.org/publications/ideas_summit/Redefining_College_Affordability.pdf: 5.

56 Ibid., 7.

57 The financial aid system is also failing because it does not account for the growing difference in the cost of living in different parts of the country. For instance, Pell Grants are not adjusted to deal with the huge difference in housing costs in Kentucky versus California or New York City.

58 Goldrick-Rab, S., and Sorenson, K. "Unmarried parents in college." *Fragile Families* 20.2 (2010): 179–203.

59 Kahlenberg, R. D. "Magnifying social inequality." *Chronicle of Higher Education July* 2 (2012): 58.

60 "Has higher education become an engine of inequality?" 2012. A forum. *The Chronicle of Higher Education,* 2 July.

61 Academe Blog. "Student debt, by the numbers: Part 2: Factors–increases in higher ed enrollment: http://academeblog.org/2012/12/05/student-debt-by-the-numbers-part-2-factors-increases-in-higher-ed-enrollment/.

62 Samuels, Robert. *Why public higher education should be free: How to decrease cost and increase quality at American Universities.* Rutgers University Press, 2013.

4

THE MYTH OF THE FAIR MERITOCRACY

Driving the public policies concerning higher education and the general economy is a set of myths regarding the fairness of the current social system. Perhaps the main myth is the idea that universities and colleges are a fair meritocracy rewarding people for their individual talents and not because of their inherited wealth or social positions.[1] However, this chapter documents how this belief in the meritocratic system blinds us from seeing the ways higher education institutions are becoming more like aristocratic societies. Instead of American colleges and universities enabling social and class mobility, they tend to enhance economic inequality and social stratification. Furthermore, the belief in the higher ed meritocratic myth helps to rationalize and justify the inequality of the larger economic system.

Higher Education's Anti-meritocracy

One reason why politicians and school officials do not see how the educational meritocracy is failing is because they are almost all winners of the system. For example, Barack Obama often relates how much of his success was due to his educational opportunities, and he believes that everyone should have the same opportunity to have their hard work rewarded with a good job. Unfortunately, as we have seen in previous chapters, college degrees do not create new good jobs, and the individual advancement of some often comes at the price of the stagnation of the many. Moreover, since institutions of higher education are very concerned about their rankings and ratings, and these ranking and rating systems favor wealthy institutions and wealthy individuals, the meritocracy has been gamed by the rich and the powerful. For instance, SAT tests were developed to provide an even playing field for students from all over the country to be held to the same standard; however, we know that this meritocratic test tends to reinforce class privilege since high scores are greatly correlated with the wealth of the parents.[2] The reason for this correlation may be that these students attended better high schools or they were given better test preparation or their parents are highly educated; although it is hard to determine what the main factor is for this correlation between wealth and test scores, we do know about some of the effects of this connection. Not only do high SAT scores help students get into colleges and universities with high graduation rates, but high SAT scores are also often rewarded with high-merit aid packages. Furthermore, when schools accept more wealthy students with higher SAT scores, their rankings go up, and this motivates more people to apply, which increases the school's selectivity rate and reputation factor.[3]

Perhaps the most pernicious aspect of the continuing myth that American universities and colleges are a fair meritocracy is the fact that this false belief allows people to believe that our economic and social system is just, and if people are unsuccessful or poor, it must be their own fault. After all, the educational meritocracy is a competition between individuals for a scarce resource (high grades and degrees), which necessitates that there will always be some winners and many losers, yet we know from many studies concerning wealth and privilege that the wealthy often believe that they have earned their wealth and that the system is essentially fair for everyone.[4] However, the economics of higher education tells us that the system is not fair because it does not provide equal opportunity, and it does not produce equal outcomes. Ultimately, the ideal of an educational meritocracy is a myth many politicians and citizens repeat in order to justify their own privilege and remove themselves from any responsibility for building a more just society.

THE MYTH OF THE FAIR MERITOCRACY   57

Experimenting with Meritocracy

The UC Berkeley Professor Paul Piff has developed some very interesting experiments to study wealth inequality and related issues. In one experiment, he has several pairs of people play the game Monopoly, but before the game begins, they roll the dice, and whoever gets the highest number starts off the game with twice as much money and gets to use both dice instead of one.[5] After the game, the players are interviewed, and Piff found that the people who started off with more money claim that they won because of their choices and smartness. Piff also noticed that the players who started off with an advantage tended to speak in a much more aggressive fashion, and they ate more from the free bowl of pretzels placed next to the game. In the summary of his research, Piff concluded that "As a person's levels of wealth increase, their feelings of compassion and empathy go down, and their feelings of entitlement, of deservingness, and their ideology of self-interest increase."[6] In other words, wealthy people tend to believe in a meritocracy because it justifies and rationalizes their advantages and good fortune, and at the same time, it cuts them off from others whom they see as less successful and less deserving.

In applying Piff's findings to higher education, we can see that universities are like a rigged game of Monopoly where some people start with a tremendous advantage, but everyone is treated as if they entered the game on an equal basis. Moreover, after higher education sorts people by degrees and grades and college rankings, the system is made to look fair and rational. Higher education is thus the engine of the meritocracy and a system that allows inequality to be rationalized as it sorts people into winners and losers. However, we know that wealthy people start off with a tremendous advantage when they enter higher education, and if we do not acknowledge this advantage, we as a society are placed in the position of the fortunate person who believes that all of his or her gains are based solely on individual talent.

As our society becomes more unequal, it becomes even more important for the belief in a meritocracy to make things seem fair and rational. For instance, President George W. Bush declared that income inequality is real, and it has been rising for twenty-five years; however, he added that "The reason is clear. We have an economy that increasingly rewards education and skills because of that education."[7] Therefore, even when a politician does recognize economic inequality, the cause for this problem is tied directly to education. The effect of this political myth is twofold: (1) the focus of political intervention is narrowed to a single variable, and (2) the social problem of economic inequality is equated with an individual's level of education.

As John Marsh argues in his book *Class Dismissed,*

> a surprising consensus has grown up in the United States around the belief that what causes poverty and economic inequality is a lack of education and that what will fix these ills is more and better education. Crucially, the conventional wisdom explains not just why some people get ahead, but it also justifies why some people are left behind.[8]

Marsh adds that there is a bipartisan consensus around this political myth that places education as the driving force behind both social inequality and social justice. This shared belief in the educational meritocracy not only blinds us from the other forces shaping economic life, but it also prevents us from seeing how education is itself a producer and enhancer of inequality.

While higher education is seen as the key to economic mobility, it has also been positioned as the solution to virtually every social problem. For instance, politicians and pundits from both political parties have claimed that education is the single most important way to counter poverty. Thus, Marsh quotes Nicholas Kristof who wrote that good schools "constitute a far more potent weapon against poverty than welfare, food stamps or housing subsidies."[9] There are so many problems with this claim that it is hard to know where to start. First, poverty affects who attends

THE MYTH OF THE FAIR MERITOCRACY   59

and graduates from all levels of education, and so it makes no sense to say that schooling is more important than social programs aimed at helping the poor. Second, and perhaps most important, is the notion that not only is education the solution to all social and economic problems, but it also then must be the cause. In other words, according to this set of myths, we should not focus on the job market or other economic factors; instead, we should blame our education system for poverty, unemployment, underemployment, inequality, poor health standards, and inflation.

As Marsh highlights, making matters worse is the rhetoric of globalization, which tends to increase the pressure on schools to help America as a nation and Americans as individuals compete in the international economic system. Thus, President Obama stated in 2009 that "in a global economy where the most valuable skill you can sell is your knowledge, a good education is no longer just a pathway to opportunity—it is a prerequisite."[10] This very common argument is based on a series of political myths regarding education, inequality, and jobs. The central myth is that one's education is equal to one's skill level and economic productivity. In what is commonly called the human capital argument, the idea is that employers pay workers for the employee's skills, and these skills are determined by one's level of education.[11] Yet, a question that should be asked is what happened to the skill level of all of the workers in Detroit when the car industry collapsed? Did the workers suddenly lose their skills, and did technological advances make their education level no longer appropriate? In fact, if we look at all of the manufacturing jobs that have been lost due to globalization, outsourcing, and automation, we find that the determining factor has been the quest to produce the same product at a lower cost. Massive unemployment was not caused by workers no longer having the degrees or skills to do the job; instead, free trade agreements and technological developments helped employers save money by automating and offshoring labor.[12] These foreign workers who are replacing American workers do not have more education; in fact, what helps to rationalize

60　THE MYTH OF THE FAIR MERITOCRACY

the low pay in other countries is the lack of education of the workers. It is also questionable whether these foreign workers have more knowledge or better skills, but that does not stop companies from outsourcing and offshoring to save money and to avoid taxes and regulations.

Moreover, if higher education does indeed make people more critical and creative thinkers, this is probably the last thing that many employers want workers to learn. The whole myth of the knowledge economy is based on a false idea that most of the jobs today are centered on creating and analyzing information, when in reality, most jobs are in the service and retail areas. By focusing on the skills and education of the workers, we fail to see how multinational companies have shifted millions of jobs from the United States to other countries, and virtually none of this had to do with the educational levels of our workers. According to a report by Working America,

> Manufacturing employment collapsed from a high of 19.5 million workers in June 1979 to 11.5 million workers in December 2009, a drop of 8 million workers over 30 years. Between August 2000 and February 2004, manufacturing jobs were lost for a stunning 43 consecutive months—the longest such stretch since the Great Depression.

During this same period of job loss, "U.S. multinational corporations, the big brand-name companies that employ a fifth of all American workers ... cut their work forces in the U.S. by 2.9 million ... while increasing employment overseas by 2.4 million."[13] It should be obvious that between 2000 and 2004, millions of American workers did not suddenly lose their education and skills; rather, companies downsized their own workers and sought out a better labor deal elsewhere.

Outsourcing and offshoring make a mockery out of the meritocratic idea that education is the single most important thing determining the future earnings of a worker. For instance, although new high-tech, knowledge-based companies are increasing their

THE MYTH OF THE FAIR MERITOCRACY 61

economic activity and profits, the manufacturing of electronics is done mostly by uneducated, low-paid workers in the Third World.[14] Moreover, as former middle-class jobs get outsourced, people with only high school degrees see their income levels decrease. This helps to increase the college premium—not by raising the compensation of the people with college degrees, but by lowering the income of the people without college degrees.

Instead of looking at economic factors like outsourcing and tax evasion, pundits and political officials continue to stress education as the key to every social issue. For instance, Marsh cites a *New York Times* article from economist Tyler Cowan who in 2007 proclaimed that "the most commonly cited culprits for income inequality in America—outsourcing, immigration, and gains of the super-rich—are diversions from the main issue. Instead, the problem is largely one of a (lack of) education."[15] Here, we enter the heart of the political motivations behind the educational and meritocratic myths: people with wealth and power do not want the public to spend a lot of time thinking about outsourcing or the super-rich; instead, in an act of misdirection, all of the attention is placed on education.

It is interesting that in Marsh's analysis of how our investment in the educational meritocracy blinds us from seeing the real forces behind social and economic inequality, he constantly cites economists who work at universities. The stress on education as a solution to every economic problem can be in part blamed on the fact that highly educated people working at educational institutions are often the ones making these claims. It thus seems natural for them to insist that higher education is the key to economic mobility, but one has to ask why these economists don't notice that their own institutions have replaced secure, high-paying professors with part-time, low-wage adjunct faculty.[16] Perhaps their investment in the educational meritocracy has multiple functions: (1) it serves to justify their own relative privilege, (2) it promotes further investment in their own institutions, and (3) it allows them to ignore the exploitation of academic workers that helps to fund their own privileged positions.

Economists then are motivated to see higher education as a fair meritocracy and the solution to all of our problems.

Rationalizing Inequality

According to Thomas Frank, since the payoff for a college degree is going up on average, institutions of higher education know that they can increase the price of admission, and people will continue to apply, especially at selective schools. The flip side of this system is that non-wealthy people also need to go to college, even if they cannot afford it, in order to compete for decent jobs:

> Although a college degree doesn't necessarily guarantee a life of splendor, not having one pretty much makes a life of poorly compensated toil a sure thing. Finding ourselves on the receiving end of inequality is a fate we will pay virtually any price to avoid, and our system of higher ed exists to set and extract that price.[17]

The logic here is the inverse of the myth that states that a college degree is the ticket to a good job; instead, the lack of a college degree sets a young person up for a life of rationalized poverty.

According to Frank, the increased connection between degrees and jobs has transformed a previous public good into a private one:

> Everyone in the age of inequality knows that the purpose of a college education isn't to benefit the nation; it's to give the private individual a shot at achieving a High Net Worth. Agreeing upon that, everyone from state legislators to the Secretary of Education naturally began to ask, Why should I pay for someone else to get rich? Those people need to foot the bill themselves.[18]

In a strange paradoxical way, the more the rewards for college degrees have become unequal, the more it becomes a private good, and the less states want to support public institutions. Here, the meritocracy undermines both the equality of opportunity and

THE MYTH OF THE FAIR MERITOCRACY   63

the equality of outcomes: the wealthy have an advantage in attending and graduating from college, and this advantage is correlated with increased wealth and better jobs. Therefore, due to the inequality of results, everyone else is forced to compete for a piece of the shrinking meritocratic pie.

Frank adds that the more a society becomes unequal and the higher the payoff for a college degree, the more universities and colleges can charge: "Agreeing upon that, the colleges and universities reconceived their mission and began to put a more accurate price tag on what the consensus now acknowledged that they were selling."[19] Since colleges are no longer selling education or citizenship and are instead selling an individual ticket to a potential life of wealth, selective schools can price the ticket for entry to a rate worthy of the upper class. As Frank adds,

> College is where money and merit meet; where the privileged learn that they are not only smarter than everyone else but that they are more virtuous, too. They are better people with better test scores, better taste, better politics. College itself is the biggest lesson of them all, the thing that teaches us where we stand in a world that is very rapidly coming apart.[20]

The real college premium, therefore, is a meritocratic rationalization of class privilege and its role in the general economy.

The Ideology of Meritocracy

In his book, *Twilight of the Elites: America after Meritocracy*, Christopher Hayes discusses many of the key reasons why our current meritocracy no longer functions like a true meritocratic system.[21] One of his main points is that the wealthy have learned how to game the system, and so the inequality of outcomes has overrun the equality of opportunity, but people still want to believe that the system is fair. Moreover, we continue to think that experts should rule the world, and this expertise is validated by higher education.[22] To prove this point, Hayes turns to the Obama administration as an example of a group of meritocratic elites who are

64 THE MYTH OF THE FAIR MERITOCRACY

all part of the same social network of power.[23] Hayes adds that Obama's belief in his own story makes him believe that the system still works.[24] However, the general public is increasingly aware that the political system itself is being controlled by the rich and powerful, and so the link between democracy and meritocracy is being weakened.

One of the main points of Hayes' book is that in all of our current systems of meritocracy—from athletics to education—there is a growing awareness of cheating and unfairness, and yet we still want to believe in the idea of a fair meritocracy. It as if we know the game is fixed, but since it is the only game in town, we try to pretend that it is still fair and rational. For Hayes, one of the political effects of this continued investment in the ideology of meritocracy is that group-based politics is replaced by a focus on individual achievement.[25] He adds that this meritocratic ideology combines the Left's concern to overcome the old aristocracy with the Right's belief in a social hierarchy.[26] In short, one reason why there is a bipartisan consensus around seeing education as the solution to economic and social inequality is that this meritocratic system supposedly moves away from a structure of inherited wealth to one of economic opportunity by sorting people by their talent and skills. However, as we have seen, the educational system is itself shaped by wealth, and the idea of a level playing field is an ideological myth.

Hayes points out that a meritocracy naturally turns into an oligarchy because those who climb up the ladder pull it up after they reach the top.[27] In higher education, we see a great example because the tenure-track professors are often called "ladder-rank" faculty in order to stress how they have a career with a clear process for advancement. Yet, the vast majority of the faculty are no longer on this career ladder, and so we have a situation where the people who have climbed up the meritocratic pecking order have taken the ladder with them. These same faculty then have to rationalize their privilege by stressing the meritocratic nature of higher education. In other terms, at the very moment when the system no longer functions, the people who

THE MYTH OF THE FAIR MERITOCRACY 65

have profited from the system have to pretend that it still works. Hayes affirms that as a meritocracy sorts people into winners and losers, the winners still compete in the system because there is always someone else ahead of them. The psychological effect of this structure is that the winners are often both highly arrogant and highly insecure.[28] Furthermore, this type of meritocracy feeds a capitalistic logic of endless competition between isolated individuals and is thus fundamentally antisocial.

In what is called "insecure self-esteem," everyone becomes obsessed about how they rank and rate in comparison to everyone else. In fact, we see that many colleges and universities are dominated by this mindset, which forces them to compete in the college rankings race even though they know this system is unfair and has nothing to do with educational quality. Meritocracy therefore breeds institutional narcissism, which combines an intense focus on the self with an obsessional need to be validated by others. This type of meritocratic narcissism also produces an ideology of cynical conformity where everyone tries to outcompete everyone else in a system in which no one believes.

Hayes argues that driving this social rat race is the notion that smartness is the top quality that a meritocracy judges, and we continue to believe that we know how to define, rank, and rate intelligence.[29] Education then plays a key role in this social system because it is in the arena of education that the mythic belief in intelligence testing is perpetuated. Since we believe that we can test and grade individual talent and skill, and translate a quality into a quantity, we believe in the rationality and the fairness of the meritocratic system.

Sorting vs. Learning

Education in America has always been caught between the dueling functions of learning and social sorting. In this structure, teachers are not only supposed to help students learn, but they also have to assess and grade their students on a regular basis. One of the problems here is that teaching and grading are two very different activities, and they are often in conflict with each other.[30] For instance, in order to learn, one has to acknowledge what one does not know and be willing to take risks in order to find new solutions; however, grading can make students risk averse as it motivates them to rely on their old knowledge and not try out new things. Grading also turns a classroom into a competition between individuals for a scarce resource, and therefore collaboration and social learning are undermined.

Since grades are an external reward, many students have been trained to only care about extrinsic rewards and not internal motivations. This system of socialization results in what is called *cynical conformity*: people learn to compete in a system in which they do not believe, and this is what we are seeing in the case of our current meritocracy.[31] From a cynical perspective, cynical conformity is not a bad thing because we all have to do things we do not want to do in society, and so it is better if people do not base their actions on internal beliefs or values. In fact, David Labaree argues in his *How to Succeed in School without Really Learning* that the main thing students learn in education is how to work the system.

Notes

1 For the original theory of the meritocracy, see Michael Dunlop Young. *The rise of the meritocracy*. Transaction Publishers, 1958.

2 Rampell, Catherine. "SAT scores and family income." *New York Times* (2009). http://economix.blogs.nytimes.com/2009/08/27/sat-scores-and-family-income/.

3 "Why US News College rankings hurt students." www.cbsnews.com/news/why-us-news-college-rankings-hurt-students/.

4 Kraus, Michael W., and Dacher Keltner. "Social class rank, essentialism, and punitive judgment." *Journal of Personality and Social Psychology* 105.2 (2013): 247.

5 Paul Piff. TED Talk: www.ted.com/talks/paul_piff_does_money_make_you_mean.

6 Ibid.

7 Marsh, John. *Class dismissed: Why we cannot teach or learn our way out of inequality*. NYU Press, 2012: 13.

8 Ibid.

9 Ibid., 14–15.

10 Ibid., 14.

THE MYTH OF THE FAIR MERITOCRACY 67

11 Blundell, Richard, et al. "Human capital investment: The returns from education and training to the individual, the firm and the economy." *Fiscal Studies* 20.1 (1999): 1–23.

12 Lach, Alex. "5 Facts about overseas outsourcing." Center for American Progress. July 9, 2012. Accessed April 28, 2013. www.americanprogress.org/issues/labor/news/2012/07/09/11898/5-facts-about-overseas-outsourcing/.

13 Ibid.

14 Birdsall, Nancy. "Life is unfair: Inequality in the world." *Foreign Policy* (1998): 76–93.

15 Marsh, 15.

16 Colander, David, et al. "The financial crisis and the systemic failure of the economics profession." *Critical Review* 21.2–3 (2009): 249–267.

17 Frank, Thomas. "Colleges are full of it: Behind the three-decade scheme to raise tuition, bankrupt generations, and hypnotize the media." www.salon.com/2014/06/08/colleges_are_full_of_it_behind_the_three_decade_scheme_to_raise_tuition_bankrupt_generations_and_hypnotize_the_media/.

18 Ibid.

19 Ibid.

20 Ibid.

21 Hayes, Christopher. *Twilight of the elites: America after meritocracy.* Random House LLC, 2013.

22 Hayes, 16.

23 Ibid., 20.

24 Ibid., 21.

25 Ibid., 47.

26 Ibid.

27 Ibid., 58.

28 Ibid., 162.

29 Ibid., 164.

30 Elbow, Peter. "Embracing contraries in the teaching process." *College English* (1983): 327–339.

31 Caldwell, Raymond. "Is anyone listening? Communicating change to employees." *Strategic Change* 2.2 (1993): 83–87; Phenix, Philip H. "Liberal learning and the practice of freedom." *The Christian Scholar* (1967): 6–26; and Callan, Eamonn. "When to shut students up: Civility, silencing, and free speech." *Theory and Research in Education* 9.1 (2011): 3–22.

5

HOW COLLEGE CHANGED CHILDHOOD, EDUCATION, AND PARENTING IN AMERICA

Due in part to the unequal distribution of the college payoff and the high selectivity of elite institutions, many parents now believe that one of their main tasks is to get their kids into the "best" colleges. This focus on admissions to select schools has warped many aspects of our society, but it is in the realm of parenting where we see some of the most pernicious effects. Not only are parents relying on false and misleading information regarding the relation between jobs and degrees, but they are also turning inequality and social mobility into a highly private matter. Therefore, instead of spending their energies on trying to make our economic and educational systems more equal and fair, parents and children are trying to outcompete everyone else. As a classic case of the tragedy of the commons, where each individual thinks only about getting the most out of a shrinking resource, everyone ends up losing.

Beating the Birth Lottery

Although parents think that they can will their children into the best schools by driving them from one scheduled activity to the next, what we know about college admissions tells us that the future educational possibilities of many children are decided at birth. The sad reality is that most elite institutions only cater to kids coming from the wealthiest families, and all levels of education are structured by class and race differences. However, many middle-class parents still want their children to go to selective universities, and so the competition for a small number of

How College Changed Childhood

elite openings only increases the pressure that each parent and child feels. Furthermore, as the price of college attendance continues to increase, more parents push their children to become excellent in an extracurricular activity that will hopefully earn their child a needed scholarship. The end result is that we find six-year-old children being pushed into team sports since their parents believe that if their child does not outcompete everyone else, there is no way their child will earn an athletic scholarship in order to afford college.

The College-Parenting Complex

In her book review, "*How to Raise an Adult* by Julie Lythcott-Haims," Heather Havrilesky reveals how deeply the competition to get into a selective college has transformed parenting in the United States.[1] She opens her article by asking "When did the central aim of parenting become preparing children for success?"[2] This question might be so difficult for people to answer because it now seems natural for parents to see their main role as guiding their kids to a successful future, but it should be clear that this obsession of preparing young children for the future is relatively new and has to do with the changing nature of degrees, jobs, and inequality. As our economy becomes increasingly unequal, the value of a college degree goes up because it is seen as the only real path to a good job and a stable future. Moreover, since the main path of advancement is perceived to be the education meritocracy, parents see it as their mission to get their children to focus on developing their individual talents as these young people work to receive high grades in school. From Havrilesky's perspective,

> This reigning paradigm, which dictates that every act of nurturing be judged on the basis of whether it will usher a child toward a life of accomplishment or failure, embodies the fundamental insecurity of global capitalist culture, with its unbending fixation on prosperity and the future. It's no surprise that parenting incites such heated debates, considering

70 HOW COLLEGE CHANGED CHILDHOOD

how paradoxical these principles can be when they're applied to children. When each nurturing act is administered with the distant future in mind, what becomes of the present? A child who soaks in the ambient anxiety that surrounds each trivial choice or activity is an anxious child, formed in the hand-wringing, future-focused image of her anxious parents.[3]

This focus on the future of children is therefore making parents and kids anxious, and it is often driven by the mistaken belief that if one does not get into the best school, then one's life is over. In this cultural context, childhood becomes a form of training and testing as parents seek to determine whether their children will do well in the future.

Havrilesky posits that as the competition to get into elite universities increases, and society becomes more unequal, middle-class parents have adopted a much more invasive model of parenting:

Caught up in what the author calls the 'college admissions arms race,' parents treat securing their children a spot at one of 20 top schools (as decreed by U.S. News and World Report's popular but somewhat dubious rankings) as an all-or-nothing proposition. Concerned about the effects of a flawed high school transcript, parents do their children's homework, write or heavily edit their papers, fire questions at teachers, dispute grades and hire expensive subject tutors, SAT coaches and 'private admissions consultants' (26 percent of college applicants reported hiring these in 2013).[4]

Driving this form of parenting is the idea that parents can and should determine the future success of their children, and higher education is the main vehicle for this success.

The anxiety caused by economic inequality and competitive college admissions reaches down and affects many aspects of the relation between children and their parents:

Whether a child is learning to ride a bike or doing his own laundry, he is still viewed through the limited binary lens of either triumphant or fumbling adulthood. The looming question is

HOW COLLEGE CHANGED CHILDHOOD 71

not "Is my child happy?" but "Is my child a future president poised to save the environment, or a future stoner poised to watch his fifth episode of 'House of Cards' in a row?'".[5]

Like Christians in premodern Europe looking for signs of pre-destination, parents today feel that they need to constantly monitor and judge the abilities of their children to see if they are making progress toward the desired goal of getting into a good college. From this perspective, the increased emphasis on testing children in K-12 is matched by the enhanced meritocratic judging of kids by parents.

According to Lythcott-Haims, "We speak of dreams as boundless, limitless realms … but in reality often we create parameters, conditions and limits within which our kids are permitted to dream—with a checklisted childhood as the path to achievement."[6] Perhaps parents have always wanted the best for their children, but now the definition of the best is narrowly defined by middle-class parents as being accepted into a high-ranked university. Of course, the first problem with these beliefs surrounding college is that many people who do not go to the most selective colleges have a successful life, and going to an elite school does not guarantee a life of happiness. More importantly, there is now evidence that the pressure to get into a selective college is harming the mental health of children and parents:

> a 2011 study by sociologists at the University of Tennessee at Chattanooga that found a correlation, in college-student questionnaires, between helicopter parenting and medication for anxiety or depression. One researcher at a treatment center for addicts in Los Angeles found that 'rates of depression and anxiety among affluent teens and young adults … correspond to the rates of depression and anxiety suffered by incarcerated juveniles.' Other studies suggest that overparented kids are 'less open to new ideas' and take 'less satisfaction in life.'[7]

Although the concept of helicopter parenting will be questioned below, there is a great deal of educational research that shows

72 HOW COLLEGE CHANGED CHILDHOOD

that some current college students often have a hard time learning new and different ideas and information because they are so concerned about maintaining their self-image of being a good student. In turn, parents themselves often judge the success of their parenting based on whether their children get into a "good" school or not.

As Havrilesky points out, many parents now see the problems stemming from the over-investment in a child's training for future success, but they are afraid to stop competing in the college rat race because they do not want to fall behind the other competitive parents:

> this emphasis on giving kids a little more space hasn't seemed to have had much effect on the premature apprehension of the schoolyard: the endless, nervous chatter about the Common Core, the uneasy comparing of report cards and standardized test scores, the tireless griping about the never-ending hassles of homework, soccer season, piano lessons, art classes, dance classes and Kumon tutoring. If everyone agrees that overscheduling and multiple hours of homework a night are the enemy, shouldn't more parents be stepping back and relaxing a little, thereby showing, by example, how to live in a nonsensically competitive world and still be happy?[8]

Since so many middle-class parents are conforming to the same competitive mindset, they overschedule their kids even if they see it may be harmful.

Driving this parental conformity is their desire to guide their child into being admitted into the "best" college:

> Lythcott-Haims sees this inability to disengage as a side effect of the prevailing fantasy among parents that the "right" college education will secure a child's comfy seat in the upper-middle-class tax bracket. Parents are so laser-focused on how to ensure success against a backdrop of an increasingly insecure global economy that they're willing to trade in the joys and self-guided discoveries of a rich childhood for some

promise of security in the far-off future. But it's absurd for parents to allow this illusion that success in life depends on admission to one of a handful of elite colleges to guide their behavior from the time their kids are in preschool forward.[9]

We see here how the competition to get into the most highly ranked colleges has transformed one of the most fundamental institutions of human civilization: the family.

Meritocratic Parenting and Educating

The effects of the college admission rates, growing inequality, and meritocratic thinking on American parenting have also been explored in depth by Alfie Kohn in his book *The Myth of the Spoiled Child*.[10] One of his central claims is that the focus on education as the solution to all of our social and economic problems represents one of the only beliefs showing widespread agreement on the Left and the Right:

> Have a look at the unsigned editorials in left-of-center news-papers, or essays by columnists whose politics are mostly progressive. Listen to speeches by liberal public officials. On any of the controversial issues of our day, from tax policy to civil rights, you'll find approximately what you'd expect. But when it comes to education, almost all of them take a hard-line position very much like what we hear from conservatives. They endorse a top-down, corporate-style version of school reform that includes prescriptive, one-size-fits-all teaching standards and curriculum mandates; weakened job protection for teachers; frequent standardized testing; and a reliance on rewards and punishments to raise scores on those tests and compel compliance on the part of teachers and students.[11]

Like the parental focus on making sure that their children are progressing toward the final goal of attaining admission to a great college, politicians and the general public have bought into the myth that the best way to prepare young people for the future is to constantly test, grade, and rank them.

74 HOW COLLEGE CHANGED CHILDHOOD

For Kohn, underlying the progressive investment in educational achievement is a conservative myth that the key to success is self-discipline. According to this conservative mantra, "What young people need—and lack—is not self-esteem but self-discipline: the ability to defer gratification, control their impulses, and persevere at tasks over long periods of time."[12] While parents are now being told that they must help their children develop self-discipline so that they can survive in a competitive world, this mindset is being shaped by the combination of social Darwinism, austerity politics, and competitive capitalism. As Kohn insists, much of this logic is driven by a few basic rules derived from a misreading of human psychology. These common myths argue:

> that rewards are necessary to motivate people, that these rewards should be made artificially scarce and given only to winners, and that the best way to prepare children for future unhappiness and failure is to make them experience unhappiness and failure right now.[13]

As it becomes harder to get into selective colleges and the employment market for good jobs shrinks, parents have learned to train their children to fight for the few remaining rewards of an unequal society. The popular myths about degrees, jobs, and inequality thus reach down to the most fundamental levels of society as children from an early age are socialized to see economic disparities as opportunities for individual advancement rather than social change.

Driving part of this social movement is the notion that our country will never become more just and equal, and we will always be fighting over a diminishing amount of rewards, and so only the fittest people will survive the harsh meritocratic competition. In this social structure, the parents' role is to train their children to outcompete other children, and this parental training is performed through a careful system of rewards and punishments. Kohn adds that this model of parenting is political and is not based on sound scientific evidence:

HOW COLLEGE CHANGED CHILDHOOD

Even though these assumptions prove false, each of them is driven by an ideological conviction that cannot be unseated by evidence—namely, that anything desirable should have to be earned (conditionality), that excellence can be attained only by some (scarcity), and that children ought to have to struggle (deprivation).[14]

Ultimately what Kohn is showing is how the logic of meritocratic capitalism is now reshaping all of our fundamental social relationships: not only are schools constantly paying students off through grades, but parents are also seeing every interaction as an opportunity to either reward or punish their kids by making rationed parental love conditioned on the successful completion of desired activities.

For Kohn, the flipside of constantly judging, rewarding, and punishing children is that young people are denied a chance to simply enjoy life and develop a positive sense of their own selves: "What provokes particular outrage and ridicule is the idea that children might feel good about themselves in the absence of impressive accomplishments, even though, as I'll show, studies find that unconditional self-esteem is a key component of psychological health."[15] In a society where everything must be earned, and rewards are becoming scarce, children are trained to only value meritocratic success.

In many ways, children are now being socialized from a very early age to adapt to a neoliberal economic order and not to try to make society more just and productive. The keys to this worldview are the acceptance that profits (rewards) will always be given to a few at the top, and we must reduce our support to other people because we can no longer afford to help others. Behind this seemingly natural economic structure is the successful implementation of a set of public policies dedicated to increasing the wealth of a relatively small number of elites. Starting in the 1970s, not only have we witnessed a disconnect between median wages and productivity, but we have also seen a tax revolt by the richest Americans and the associated reduction of public support for higher education, welfare assistance,

76   HOW COLLEGE CHANGED CHILDHOOD

and other social programs. Part of this neoliberal logic is derived from the policies of the World Bank and the IMF, which
were originally applied to Third World developing nations. In
response to growing debt and stagnant economic development,
international organizations forced poor countries to privatize
their industries, open themselves up to external investment,
and cut their support for public institutions.[16] Although many of
these policies failed, the same ideas are now being applied to the
most developed nations. For example, after the Great Recession
of 2008–2009, many wealthy Western nations reduced spending
on public services, which drove up the costs for higher education
and eliminated many welfare state benefits.[17] This austerity re-
gime was in part based on the idea that we can no longer afford
to help people in need, but we have to find ways to increase the
wealth of the people at the top. What Kohn then helps to reveal
is how this neoliberal logic has also been restructuring parenting and education.

For Kohn, a major paradox is that many people now feel that
schools and parents are failing our children because these social
institutions have become too lax, and yet any careful analysis
of education and parenting today actually shows that adults are
imposing a lifestyle on children that undermines the independence and involvement of young people:

> The idea that we live in a permissive or child-centered culture
> also seems unshaken despite what things are like for children at
> school, where they spend a significant portion of their waking
> hours. There, a variety of behavior management programs—
> consisting of some version of bribes and threats—are employed
> to make students comply with rules that they almost certainly
> had no role in helping to formulate. The emphasis is not on
> promoting moral development but on eliciting compliance.
> More broadly, John Dewey's characterization of most schools
> remains accurate today: The 'center of gravity' is outside the
> child. We say, in effect: This is the curriculum; this is how we
> will evaluate you; these are our rules and requirements, all of

them having been set up long before we met you. Your needs and interests—or even those of an entire class—will have no bearing on what we do and what we demand.[18]

From this perspective, school undermines democracy because it imposes a set curriculum supported by a strict system of rewards and punishment, which negates the involvement and power of individual students. Therefore, as kids are trained to respond to a capitalist system of scarce rewards, they are also excluded from democratic participation in the formation of their own education.

In light of these changing attitudes about education and parenting, we should not be surprised if our society accepts a concentration of income at the top and a decrease in effective democracy: we are essentially socializing children to be undemocratic capitalistic competitors, and we are doing this because we believe that the best way to prepare them for the future is to put private concerns over public matters as we impose a standardized model of education and parenting that undermines self-esteem and critical thinking. In terms of K-12 education, much of this neoliberal ideology is being driven by a lack of public funding combined with a misguided theory of motivation:

> Some of this is obviously a function of having twenty or thirty kids in a room and of the time and effort required to create a 'learner-centered' environment. But not all of it can be explained that way, particularly since some teachers and schools have shown that it is possible to proceed more by asking than telling. Rather, there is an ideology at work here that's similar to our approach to parenting—one defined by a fundamental lack of respect for children, by puritanical beliefs about the benefits of frustration and failure, by the assumption that children are best prepared for future unpleasantness by subjecting them to unpleasantness while they're small, and by a view of human nature that implies little can be accomplished without employing rewards and punishments as inducements to learn or to treat others kindly.[19]

78   HOW COLLEGE CHANGED CHILDHOOD

Even though there is a great deal of research on how using external rewards to motivate people often results in a loss of individual motivation, the neoliberal logic of rationing resources has found its way into the most basic forms of human interaction. Furthermore, a conservative religious ideology of learning through pain and punishment is now being combined with a liberal philosophy of meritocratic judgment.

This bipartisan consensus about education and parenting reveals how powerful neoliberal ideology has become since this often unconscious belief system has helped to transform the way people now see their relations to everyone else around them:

> It's also possible that self-centeredness is connected to the extraordinary emphasis on achievement and winning in contemporary America: schooling that's focused on mastering a series of narrowly defined academic skills in rapid succession, that's measured by nearly continuous standardized testing, that leaches from the school day into the evening with copious amounts of homework, and that's defined by a desperate competition for awards, distinctions, and admission to selective colleges, the point being not merely to do well but to triumph over everyone else.[20]

Many studies have shown that as societies become more unequal, social trust is reduced, and people have a hard time understanding why they should care about the plight of others. In the case of education, the more the individual monetary payoff for college is promoted, the more it becomes a private good, and the less willing people are to support public institutions.

Kohn's focus on how parenting styles have political and social effects helps to reverse the movement from the public to the private; instead of seeing parenting as a purely private matter, he points to how our relationship with children is shaped by larger cultural forces:

> If you were to make an argument against doing-to parenting, it's unlikely that someone would challenge you by asking, 'But if we stopped using rewards and punishments, how could we

HOW COLLEGE CHANGED CHILDHOOD

make sure that our kids will be happy, psychologically healthy, genuinely concerned about others, critical thinkers who will fight against injustice and work for social change?' Instead, you would probably hear, 'No rewards and punishments?? Then how will we get our kids to do what they're told, follow the rules, and take their place in a society where certain things will be expected of them whether they like it or not?'[21]

Our investment in using rewards and punishments to shape children's behavior is so ingrained that we cannot imagine another way of doing things, and yet we are often teaching young people to simply comply with authority figures and not examine in a critical way the social world around them.

At the same time that some parents are castigated for being too lax, there is also the common perception that parents are now too involved in their children's lives. Kohn believes that one explanation for this contradiction is that our society often confuses concern with a loss of individual autonomy:

> So why is disproportionate attention paid to the possibility of being too close? It could be due to the premium that our culture places on the value of self-sufficiency. We are deeply attached to the idea of not being too attached. We see creativity as a characteristic of separate selves rather than groups, and the heroes glorified in popular culture are mostly loners. Inevitably this value system colors our approach to parenting.[22]

As we socialize children to see the world in terms of isolated individuals, we also seek to control their behavior in a controlling way:

> In *The Psychology of Parental Control*, psychologist Wendy Grolnick reports that 'controlling parenting has been associated with lower levels of intrinsic motivation, less internalization of values and morals, poorer self-regulation, and higher levels of negative self-related [emotions].' When parents are

80   HOW COLLEGE CHANGED CHILDHOOD

controlling about their children's academic performance, the effects on the children's achievement—and on their interest in learning—are usually detrimental.[23]

Once again, parenting and teaching have a similar set of problems in our neoliberal society: since we have bought into the power of external rewards, we support a system of external control, which, in turn, can undermine motivation, ethical behavior, and positive self-regard.

Controlling children through rewards and punishment may appear to be an easier way of interacting with them, yet several studies have shown that this type of relationship not only causes stress and depression, but it also does not necessarily help with grades:

> a study of Chinese-American families published in 2013, which found that children raised by 'tiger' parents (characterized by extreme control and a relentless demand for high achievement) were more likely than those raised by more supportive parents to be depressed, to describe themselves as pressured, and to feel resentment toward their parents. They also ended up having lower grades.[24]

Once again, the belief that children have to excel at an early age at everything in order to get into a good college pushes parents to undermine the mental health of the children they are trying to guide.

Kohn's insights into parenting and education challenge many of our deepest feelings about how to interact with children, and our resistance to listen to his analysis may be in part due to how deeply the neoliberal meritocratic ideology has seeped into our minds. For example, the following passage challenges many middle-class practices we see all around us today:

> Psychologically controlling parents don't just coerce children to make them act (or stop acting) in a particular way; they attempt to take over their children's very selves. Kids

HOW COLLEGE CHANGED CHILDHOOD 81

are made to feel guilty when they do something contrary to the parent's wishes. Love and acceptance are made contingent on pleasing the parent. Care, in effect, is turned into 'positive reinforcement.' When the child is well behaved or impressive, there are plenty of hugs, smiles, high-fives, and 'Good job!'s. But when the child doesn't do what the parent wants, the love is withdrawn and the atmosphere turns chilly. This strategy can be diabolically effective because the child becomes, in effect, a wholly owned subsidiary of the parent. It's harder to fight this than it is to rebel against the overt regulation of one's behavior.[25]

The key to the analysis here is the way emotional manipulation is tied to political and ideological values: we praise children and tell them how great they are, but then make them feel bad when they are not successful since we think we can train them to become successful students.

The psychological factors that Kohn analyzes are important to think about because there will be no chance of changing our society and reducing inequality if we don't first change how we view our most basic social relationships. Just as we now talk about *earning* grades, we also talk about *earning* a parent's love and respect. Here, the unconditional relationship has been transformed into a capitalist exchange: one has to prove oneself to an authority figure in order to receive a scarce resource. Sometimes, the resource is love, and other times, it is attention, but the main point is that one is constantly worried about losing the valued reward. This consumerist attitude stems from the fact that parents often see themselves through the accomplishment of their children: "two studies have found that parents whose feelings of self-worth varied with their kids' successes were apt to be more controlling than other parents, particularly if they had reason to expect their children would be judged."[26] In other words, some parents control their kids because they want their children to be praised by other people, and one reason they want this positive feedback for their children is that it reflects back on the parent. Thus, parents may push their children to get into an elite college because it makes the parents look good—not only in the eyes of others but also in their own self-perceptions.

Instead of controlling our children, Kohn makes a difficult call for unconditional love, and one thing that makes this call so hard to accept is that it goes against many of the neoliberal myths regarding parenting and education:

> When it's a struggle 'to figure out what it means to be an adult in a world of disappearing jobs, soaring education costs and shrinking social support networks,' a close connection to the people who raised you can be vital. Yet mass-media accounts continue to portray that connection as objectionable.[27]

From Kohn's perspective, we need supportive parents more than ever because the education and employment worlds have become so insecure, while the safety net is in tatters.

In relation to higher education, Kohn adds that colleges now often try to impose a white middle-class value of forced independence on students, which in many cases conflicts with the values of minority students:

> A fascinating series of studies published in 2012 by a multi-university research team revealed that 'predominantly middle-class cultural norms of independence that are institutionalized in many American colleges and universities' are particularly ill suited for young adults who are the first in their families to attend college. These norms 'do not match the relatively interdependent norms to which many first-generation students are regularly exposed in their local working-class contexts prior to college.' The result of this mismatch is to create a hidden academic disadvantage for these students, one that adversely affects their performance. Given the expectations of self-sufficiency that permeate our institutions—'learn to do for yourself'—connections with, support from, and maybe even interventions by parents become that much more important to help students.[28]

HOW COLLEGE CHANGED CHILDHOOD

Thus, instead of criticizing "helicopter" parents, Kohn thinks that parent involvement is often helpful and needed, but it has gotten a bad rap because white middle-class culture stresses individual autonomy over social relationships.

As Kohn takes on the myth of helicopter parents, he also challenges the ideas that children must learn at an early age that there are winners and losers in every social interaction:

> The argument here is that by protecting kids from unpleasantness we deprive them of beneficial experiences with failure and allow them to feel more satisfied with themselves than they deserve, thus blurring the sharp line that divides winners from losers—and excellence from mediocrity—at school and at play.[29]

In our current meritocratic culture, we are constantly ranking, grading, and testing everything, and this obsession with social sorting shapes parenting and teaching to such a degree that basic relationships and values are being undermined.

Of course, the main way this neoliberal spreading of capitalistic relations into all aspects of our lives is manifested is through our conceptions of work:

> Even our work is usually about more than just earning a living: We may complain about the daily grind, but studies show that we're often absorbed in our work and happy with it on a moment-by-moment basis. In short, regardless of age or setting, we frequently act out of curiosity or passion, animated by the sheer joy of pushing our limits or making sense of the world. Every example of this offers yet another refutation of the sad, cynical belief that people make an effort only in exchange for money, a pat on the head, or some other version of a doggie biscuit. Those who hold that belief, and consequently feel compelled to offer rewards to children, implicitly discount the power of intrinsic motivation.[30]

Kohn here links our views of education and parenting to our feelings about work, and this analysis helps us to see how effective the logic of capitalistic exchange has been in reshaping all aspects of our existence.

Just as the focus on external rewards can undermine the desire of people to learn or to be creative, the use of bonuses and other monetary rewards can hurt the motivation of workers:

> Those who defend merit pay or incentive plans in the workplace, meanwhile, apparently believe that employees could have been doing better work all along but simply refused until it was bribed out of them. A strong belief in the need to dangle rewards in front of people to 'motivate' them—or a fear of failing to do so—implies that people lack not just skills but the desire to acquire them.[31]

Since external rewards can undermine internal motivation, we may have to rethink the whole way we pay people in our current economy since many of our compensation systems are based on the premise that workers will only try at their jobs if they are bribed, and this logic also helps to structure our schools and parenting:

> Scores of studies have shown that the more you reward people for doing something, the more they tend to lose interest in whatever they had to do to get the reward. Incentives, in other words, are actually corrosive. Give a child an 'A' for learning something and he's apt to find that topic—and perhaps learning in general—a little less appealing than he did before. Offer a reward, including praise, for an act of generosity, and kids become a little less likely to help next time if they don't think they're going to get something out of it.[32]

If this theory of the negative effects of rewards is true, then our main way of parenting, teaching, and compensating people is based on a faulty theory of psychology. In fact, the external reward theory of motivation is so powerful that it is even hard to question it in public.

What then makes Kohn's book so important and so difficult to read is that it challenges our most basic assumptions about

HOW COLLEGE CHANGED CHILDHOOD 85

human behavior and how to organize a society. After all, if external rewards undermine effectiveness and motivation, then we must rethink the foundations of our schools, workplaces, and parenting. We also need to examine how we use rewards to manipulate people by creating an artificial system of scarcity:

> An award is just a reward that has been made artificially scarce: If you get one, then I can't. A good grade is a reward, and the primary effect of inducing students to try to get one is that they're less likely to ask the teacher 'What does that really mean?'[33]

Grades therefore create a permanent culture of austerity where people must compete to earn a rationed resource, and this system rarely motivates people to ask important questions or to examine information in a critical fashion.

The use of grades becomes even more pernicious when it is combined with a predetermined distribution, which is often the case in large lecture classes at American universities:

> But when students are graded on a curve, it has been decided in advance that even if all of them do well, all of them can't get A's. Now we're talking not only about extrinsic inducements (rewards) but about competition (awards). And the negative impact on learning is even more pronounced.[34]

Schools often use this system in order to "weed" students out of popular majors, but it is also utilized to turn education into a competition, and this form of competition can undermine many important aspects of learning:

> Typically, its [competition] effect is to undermine self-confidence, relationships, empathy and the inclination to help, intrinsic motivation, and, perhaps most surprisingly, excellence. Contrary to popular belief, competition usually does not enhance achievement, even on straightforward tasks. And when the tasks are more complex—for example, when they involve

creativity—study after study shows that the absence of competition is more likely to produce better results. That's true in part because a competitive environment (I can succeed only if you fail) strongly discourages the arrangement that does help people do their best: cooperation (I can succeed only if you also succeed).[35]

Once again, Kohn here questions one of the most basic myths of our neoliberal meritocracy, which is that every human activity should be turned into a competition for scarce resources. However, we know that basing education on competition instead of cooperation is not a natural development; rather, the pitting of people against each other is an artificial social construct centered on the notion that people do their best work when they have to compare themselves to other people and not when they have to work together:

When we set children against one another in contests—from spelling bees to awards assemblies to science 'fairs' (that are really contests), from dodge ball to honor rolls to prizes for the best painting or the most books read—we teach them to confuse excellence with winning, as if the only way to do something well is to outdo others.[36]

It is little wonder why so many people accept a society that generates so much inequality: after all, our education system trains people to see others as obstacles to their own success and progress.

This competitive method of schooling not only undermines social trust, but it also feeds a host of unethical behaviors:

We invite them to see their peers not as potential friends or collaborators but as obstacles to their own success. (Quite predictably, researchers have found that the results of competition often include aggression, cheating, envy of winners, contempt for losers, and a suspicious posture toward just about everyone.) Finally, we lead children to regard whatever they're doing as a means to an end: The point isn't to paint or read or design a science experiment, but to win.

The act of painting, reading, or designing is thereby devalued in the child's mind. Our culture remains in thrall to the dogma that competition builds character, that it teaches skills (which ostensibly couldn't be acquired by engaging in noncompetitive versions of the same activities), and that it motivates people to do their best.[37]

Since parents, teachers, and the media all send the same message about the importance of outcompeting others, the austerity logic of the neoliberal meritocracy breeds a culture of questionable ethical behavior.

One place where the destructive logic of testing, grading, and rating young people is the most apparent is at American high schools:

Consider the practice of ranking high school students by their grade-point averages and publicly recognizing the victor in this contest as the valedictorian. The vicious competition and resentment that ensue, as a handful of academic overachievers battle it out over tiny differences in GPA, has led some schools to identify a batch of high-scoring kids rather than a single valedictorian, or to stop ranking students entirely.[38]

Not only do some colleges now use the ranking of high school students in their admissions decisions, but many scholarships are also now connected to a student's ability to outperform fellow students. From a meritocratic perspective, this way of handing out rewards makes perfect sense and is a fair and open system. Yet, Kohn lists many reasons why awarding students with the top honor is not just or logical:

1. The differences in grade-point averages among high-achieving students are usually statistically insignificant. It's therefore both pointless and misleading to single out the 'top' student or even the ten top students. 2. Ranking students provides

88   HOW COLLEGE CHANGED CHILDHOOD

little if any practical benefit. Class rank has much less signifi-
cance to college admissions officers than does a range of other
factors, and the proportion of colleges that view it as an important consideration has been dropping steadily. As of 2005
nearly 40 percent of high schools have either stopped ranking
their students or don't share that information with colleges—
with no apparent effect on students' prospects for admission.
3. What's being rewarded isn't always merit or effort but some
combination of skill at playing the game of school (choosing
courses with a keen eye to the effect on one's GPA, figuring
out how to impress teachers, etc.) and a willingness to sacrifice sleep, health, friends, a sense of perspective, reading for
pleasure, and anything else that might interfere with one's
grades. 4. If the chance to be a valedictorian is supposed to
be a motivator, then the effect of class rank is to demotivate
the vast swath of students who realize early on that they don't
stand a chance of acquiring this distinction. 5. What we're
talking about here is extrinsic motivation, which ultimately
harms everyone, including the valedictorian. Research by educational psychologists suggests that grades typically do three
things: They reduce students' interest in learning, they lead
students to prefer less challenging tasks, and they encourage
students to think in a more superficial fashion. The effect of
class rank, honor rolls, and grade-based scholarships—all of
which are essentially rewards for having been rewarded—is
to exacerbate all three of those effects by making grades even
more salient. Pitting students against one another for the status of having the best grades adds the arsenic of competition
to the strychnine of extrinsic motivation. It not only makes
the high school experience unnecessarily stressful but simul-
taneously undermines the sense of community and support
that can help students get through those years intact.[39]

The dark side of the neoliberal meritocracy is exposed here: testing, grading, and ranking students undermine their motivation,
create an antisocial environment, and work against learning and
critical thinking. Moreover, the fundamental social institution

of the family has been reshaped by the drive for parents to out-compete each other in the effort to get their children into the best schools in a highly unequal society.

The Culture of Meritocratic Parenting

To see how all of this pressure to get into a good college is affecting children, we can look at Denise Clark Pope's *Doing School*, where she closely follows five students at a competitive high school.[40] Pope's interviews with these students are very revealing and force us to confront the question of whether our styles of parenting and teaching are actually making young people unhealthy, unethical cynical conformists: "These students explain that they are busy at what they call 'doing school.' They realize that they are caught in a system where achievement depends more on 'doing'—going through the correct motions—than on learning and engaging with the curriculum."[41] For these students, it is clear that education is no longer about learning; it is about earning grades so that they can get into the best schools: "Instead of thinking deeply about the content of their courses and delving into projects and assignments, the students focus on managing the work load and honing strategies that will help them to achieve high grades."[42] Not only are students focusing on outcompeting each other for the highest grades, but they also quickly learn how to work the system and cheat, lie, and pretend if they have to:

> They learn to raise their hands even when they don't know the answers to the teachers' questions in order to appear interested. They understand the importance of forming alliances and classroom treaties to win favors from teachers and administrators. Some feel compelled to cheat and to contest certain grades and decisions in order to get the scores they believe they need for the future.[43]

This description of student behavior makes it easy to understand how we have created a society dominated by unethical, undemocratic systems: people at a very young age are socialized to do anything they can do to compete for scarce rewards.

One of the results, then, of the way kids are being parented and taught is that they have internalized the message that it does not matter what you learn; what matters is that you outcompete others so you can get into a good college. As one student put it, "People don't go to school to learn. They go to get good grades, which brings them to college, which brings them the high-paying job, which brings them to happiness, so they think. But basically, grades is where it's at."[44] Although grades are only supposed to be a method to help teachers gauge students' progress, these quantifiable markers have become the ends and not the means. Just as money is supposed to be a means of organizing economic exchanges, making money has now become an end in itself, and in this way, grades are just another form of money.

Parents and schools then often train people to be unethical capitalists who are detached from their own activities:

> Values normally espoused in schools, such as honesty, diligence, and teamwork, necessarily come into question when the students must choose between these ideals and getting top grades. It is hard to be a team player when you are competing with peers for an A grade on the class curve. It is difficult to remain honest when so much in school depends on appearing alert and prepared, and when there is too much work to do and too little time in which to do it. The workload is so great and the expectations so high that these students feel obligated to give up recreation and sleep time as well as many aspects of a social life in order to succeed.[45]

Once again, since everyone is competing in the same system, and the system is rigged to ration out an unequal amount of rewards, neoliberal meritocratic capitalism becomes second nature, and even if the kids do not believe in the system, and they know they are forced to cheat and live an unhealthy life, they still see no other alternative:

> These students regret the frenetic pace of their school days and the undue stress they endure. They do not like

HOW COLLEGE CHANGED CHILDHOOD

manipulating the system or compromising their beliefs and values by kissing up, lying, and cheating. But they also do not like what they see as the alternative. They believe job prospects and income are better for college graduates, especially for those who earn credentials from prestigious universities. Lower grades and test scores might jeopardize future wealth and well-being. Hence, the students are victims of what I call the 'grade trap.' They feel bound by a narrow definition of success and resigned to a system in which ultimate satisfaction may not be attainable.[46]

Pope here summarizes much of what is wrong with our current society: we know that the system is unfair and unhealthy, but we do not challenge it because we are too busy trying to outperform everyone else.

One of the main points I have been making in this chapter is that our current unequal and undemocratic economic and political system is not only the result of economics and politics; rather, people are choosing on an individual level to accept an unfair and unequal system, and if we do not change this type of attitude, nothing can be improved. In other words, we are the problem, and we have bought into a system we do not trust. Of course, wealthy people have worked hard to rig the system and horde most of the profits and manipulate the political process, but we allow this to happen on a daily basis, and how we parent and educate determines how the next generation is going to respond to this system.

Pope sees these problems, and asks us to examine our basic understandings of what education should really be about:

Are we fostering an environment that promotes intellectual curiosity, cooperation, and integrity, or are our schools breeding anxiety, deception, and frustration? Are they impeding the very values they claim to embrace? Are we preparing students well for the future? Are they ready for the world of work? Are they ready to be valuable members of our society? And is this the kind of education to which we as a nation should aspire?[47]

Although it is hard to generalize about education as a whole, it does appear that many of our schools are not focusing on intellectual curiosity, cooperation, and integrity; instead, due to the emphasis on grades and college, these institutions breed dishonesty, deception, and anxiety. We are therefore producing the very society we criticize.

Several of the students Pope interviewed report that their efforts to get good grades and please their parents make them very stressed out and also make them disengaged from their course work:

> Instead of engaging with his classes, he spends most of his time trying to obtain the 'good grades' that will get him into college and thus make his parents happy. He's aware of the stress he feels and reluctantly tells me that it's 'probably beneficial,' believing that without it, he wouldn't be where he is today.[48]

Even though it seems logical that one would have to care about the content of what one is being taught in order to receive high grades, students often communicate that caring about the subject matter only gets in the way. The idea is to figure out what is going to be on the test and give back to the teacher what the teacher is expecting.

In an unequal society with diminished hopes for economic mobility, people will fight to outcompete others even if their actions defeat the purpose of their current activities. One student reflects this level of compromise in the following manner:

> He says with a sigh, 'I wish I could say I'm an individual, and I am not going to sacrifice my individuality for a grade, you know ... just write for writing's sake.' But he feels he cannot do this. Instead, he says, he 'compromises his beliefs' about good writing and tries to guess how the teacher wants the essay to be written or the test question to be answered.[49]

Students quickly learn that it does not matter what they think is right or important: what matters is what the reward-giver values

HOW COLLEGE CHANGED CHILDHOOD 93

and recognizes. In this contradictory system, the individual strives for the highest reward by sacrificing his or her individuality:

> This is, after all, a key part of what one learns in school—how to assimilate, behave according to a certain system, learn to write and think and speak the way you are taught, the way teachers, parents, and community members believe will lead to future success.[50]

All levels of society therefore reinforce the meritocratic grade trap and the quest to get into the right college.

According to Pope's interviews, even the students who are the most successful in the current system are not happy and feel disconnected from their own actions:

> Over and over again I ask Eve, 'Why are you doing this? Why push so hard?' And each time she replies with the same answer: To get into an Ivy. That's all I can think about ... to get in and become a successful $500,000-a-year doctor or engineer or whatever it is I want to be.... It's very narrow-minded for me.... I have to get accepted; then I can have a life, once I'm in.... Of this goal, Eve seems sure. However, she is less clear when she ponders the reasons behind the goal.[51]

These star students have bought into the idea that there is only one path for a happy life, and it is based on current self-denial and eventual acceptance into an Ivy League school.

In the case of this particular high-achieving student, and many others like her, the college achievement race takes a serious toll on her health:

> She explains: I sometimes have two or three days where I only get two hours of sleep per night. I see lots of my friends burned out, but I don't have time to worry about this ... It's the typical Asian way. Lots of us are getting sick, and I am addicted to coffee; actually, I prefer to say voluntarily

94   HOW COLLEGE CHANGED CHILDHOOD

dependent on caffeine. See, some people see health and happiness as more important than grades and college; I don't. I feel compelled to compete because we have a really smart class, and I am competing with them to get into college.[52]

This student is obviously undermining her own physical and mental health, but she continues to be praised by her parents, teachers, and peers, and so she continues down the path of possible self-destruction. Ultimately, this student feels like she is just a mechanical robot going through the motions:

> Her diligence and commitment may appear to be that of the ideal student, especially compared to those students who rarely do homework or show little concern for their future, but beneath the high GPA and the 'packed' resume, lies a tired and worried teenager with 'no life.'

Eve says,

> I am just a machine with no life at this place ... This school turns students into robots. I have been thinking about it a lot; I am a robot just going page by page, doing the work, doing the routine.[53]

One has to wonder if this is what schooling should really be about. Do we want to create a generation of students who strive to outcompete others but do not care about what they are doing? Is this what we want our future doctors, lawyers, politicians, and bankers to be like?

This question of what young people are really learning from their parents and teachers is important to ask after the Great Recession. After all, most people agree that one of the largest economic failures ever was driven by greed and unethical behavior, and all of the democratic institutions that were set up to stop such a crisis failed.[54] Furthermore, after people lost trillions of dollars of wealth, no one was held accountable, and after the government spent trillions on bailing out the wealthiest institutions, the rich returned to Wall Street to make even more money. While there were some protests after the financial crisis, business has returned back to usual, and almost everyone accepts the current rigged game because no one thinks there is an alternative. However, as I have been arguing, the problems run much deeper since our entire education and parenting structures favor tolerating high levels of inequality as a way to ration out meritocratic rewards in a new mode of social Darwinism. In fact, one of the star students in Pope's study turns to Darwin to understand her own life:

> In her tenth grade biology class, when Eve learned about Darwin's theory of evolution and the concept of 'survival of the fittest,' she immediately related the theory to her own life. She explains, 'I love that theory because that's the way my group of friends are.'[55]

A misreading of Darwin helps these students to see their self-sacrifice and desire to outcompete their peers as a natural instinct and not as a social construct of a very particular culture. As this student argues,

> The ones who manage to 'stay up and take as much stress as possible and still stay alive' are the most fit and 'stay on top and survive.' But the ones who can't 'take all the pressure and the intensity… They are not on top anymore.' The whole point is to 'beat each other and rise above.'[56]

Here, the meritocracy gets combined with social Darwinism and cynical conformity in a period of neoliberal austerity:

> Eve admits that such a theory seems 'harsh' and 'cruel,' but she believes that one must have this mindset in order to get into the best universities: A person who wants to go to Ivy League knows the ideal goals…. and you get so caught up in like this conflict preparing for it … that you realize, 'Oh wait I'm competing with all these other students too.' And the college can only accept a certain amount of people from a school, you know, and … so you start competing with them, kind of hiding things from them.[57]

96   HOW COLLEGE CHANGED CHILDHOOD

One might think that this extreme desire to get into Ivy League schools only affects a small part of the population, but the general push to get into a good school to get a good job in an unequal and unjust society affects almost everyone now.

In an effort to show how students from different class backgrounds are affected by the same meritocratic culture, Pope interviews Teresa, a low-income, Mexican-American student who works many hours outside of school as she tries to still get good grades to go to college. However, since her many family and work commitments keep getting in the way of her academic desires, she has to resort to behavior that she herself finds reprehensible:

> Instead of working hard to meet the challenges and becoming more motivated to learn the material, Teresa resorts to 'desperate' behavior. She cheats and commits plagiarism in order to salvage her grades. These actions cause her to feel conflicted because, on the one hand, she wants to 'concentrate on learning' and not worry about the grades, but she also wants to 'do well to go to college,' and she believes the C's and D's she is earning will hurt her chances.[58]

Like the wealthier star students, Teresa is also forced to sacrifice her values in order to earn the grades she thinks she needs to go to college:

> She knows she should be on time; she knows she should not have to resort to cheating and other dishonest behavior to do well in school. She says she doesn't like to do these things but chooses to do them anyway because she believes her college career depends on it.[59]

As another example of cynical conformity, Teresa feels that she has to be dishonest in order to compete within a system in which she does not trust or believe.

Teresa has internalized the dominant message that if you do not go to college, you are a failure:

HOW COLLEGE CHANGED CHILDHOOD

> You feel like oh if you don't get good grades, you won't go to college and all this bad stuff will happen to you—you're bad, you're stupid, that type of stuff. It just feels like if you don't get the good grades then you won't succeed in society.[60]

We see here how college has become such an important source of identity within our society: young people feel that if they are not heading to or going to college, then they are a failure and a social outcast.

At the same time that students try to do anything they can to get high grades, Pope reports that they also often try to hide any real interest they may have in what they are learning:

> She resolved to 'sit and listen quietly' and not ask too many questions in some of her classes where she might be considered a 'know-it-all.' She wasn't used to a system where students felt the need to cheat in order to get high grades, and she did not like hiding the fact that she was interested in the material and really wanted to learn, to be interactive.[61]

As we see on all levels of education, students can be quite brutal if they feel a student is trying too hard or cares too much. Thus, at the same time they are all trying to outcompete each other for grades, they are also trying to maintain an air of cool indifference.

Pope also discovers that many students who try not to cheat and do show an interest in what they are studying are also penalized by the system. Since many other students are cheating, the ones who try to do the right thing get marked down:

> Berto hopes he will eventually be rewarded for his dedication to work when he is appointed full manager, but he is frustrated that his honesty and strong work ethic make him easily exploitable. He continues to be disappointed when he tries to play by the rules but does not obtain the results he desires.[62]

98   HOW COLLEGE CHANGED CHILDHOOD

This low-income student feels that both at work and at school, his work ethic and honesty are exploited.

As Pope argues, the grading system tends to undermine the ability of people to learn and be honest:

> When so much emphasis is placed on grades and individual achievement, the system seems to breed dishonesty. Students learn to succeed by all means possible, even if this means compromising their integrity to obtain high grades. In this sense, Berto lacks the knowledge (Bourdieu [1977] for instance, might say the cultural capital) to succeed in the way he wishes in school. He respects his teachers and does not question their authority, even when they may be wrong. He believes in honest work and diligence, even when this may cause him to get lower grades than those who cheat and procrastinate. And he believes in helping others and receiving help in return, even when the system is largely based on independent work and assessment.[63]

Since the system is centered on rationing individual rewards, any attempt to help others or play by the rules can result in a disadvantage. Pope asks what are the effects of this type of system: "Why must the students feel the need to manipulate the system and devise crafty strategies to get ahead? Why must they feel compelled to betray friends and deceive teachers? Why must they compromise integrity for future success?"[64] It appears that the education structure incentivizes the same behavior we often see on Wall Street: students are rewarded for being manipulative, dishonest, aggressive, and antisocial.

It is interesting to note that these students often express that they are conflicted and internally divided about their own actions within the competitive grade culture:

> They wanted to believe that they deserved their high grades and status and that they had earned their success. They tried to justify their behavior, convince themselves that they were doing 'the right thing,' or that 'everybody' did school

this way. But they could not escape the fact that they were unhappy with their school decisions and were not content with what they believed were the limited options available to them. Most said that they wanted to 'concentrate on learning,' not worry about grades, act in ways that were authentic and did not compromise their beliefs.[65]

We shall see in the next chapter that this sense of cynical conformity and self-sacrifice has found its way into all aspects of higher education. From this functional perspective, K-12 education prepares students for college by socializing them to compete within a system in which they do not believe.

Notes

1 Havrilesky, Heather. "*How to raise an adult* by Julie Lythcott-Haims." *The New York Times.* June 15, 2015.
2 Ibid.
3 Ibid.
4 Ibid.
5 Ibid.
6 Ibid.
7 Ibid.
8 Ibid.
9 Ibid.
10 Kohn, Alfie. *The myth of the spoiled child: Challenging the conventional wisdom about children and parenting.* Da Capo Press, 2014.
11 Ibid., 2.
12 Ibid., 4.
13 Ibid., 7.
14 Ibid.
15 Ibid., 8.
16 Stiglitz, Joseph E. *Globalization and its discontents.* Vol. 500. Norton: New York, 2002.
17 Peck, Jamie, Nik Theodore, and Neil Brenner. "Neoliberalism resurgent? Market rule after the great recession." *South Atlantic Quarterly* 111.2 (2012): 265–288.
18 Kohn, 24.
19 Ibid., 24.
20 Ibid., 78.
21 Ibid., 47.
22 Ibid., 58.
23 Ibid., 61.
24 Ibid., 62.

25 Ibid.

26 Ibid., 64.

27 Ibid., 70.

28 Ibid., 73.

29 Ibid., 78.

30 Ibid., 80.

31 Ibid.

32 Ibid.

33 Ibid., 81.

34 Ibid.

35 Ibid., 82.

36 Ibid.

37 Ibid.

38 Ibid., 84.

39 Ibid., 85.

40 Pope, Denise Clark. *Doing school: How we are creating a generation of stressed out, materialistic, and miseducated students.* Yale University Press, 2001.

41 Ibid., 4.

42 Ibid.

43 Ibid.

44 Ibid.

45 Ibid.

46 Ibid., 5.

47 Ibid., 6.

48 Ibid., 9.

49 Ibid., 15.

50 Ibid.

51 Ibid., 32.

52 Ibid., 34.

53 Ibid., 37.

54 Scheer, Robert. *The great American stickup: How Reagan Republicans and Clinton Democrats enriched Wall Street while mugging main street.* Nation Books, 2010.

55 Pope, 37.

56 Ibid.

57 Ibid., 38.

58 Ibid., 71.

59 Ibid., 74.

60 Ibid., 82.

61 Ibid., 83.

62 Ibid.

63 Ibid.

64 Ibid., 150.

65 Ibid., 85.

6

TRAINING UNDEMOCRATIC CAPITALISTS

This chapter deals with the myth that institutions of higher education focus on teaching students how to think critically and become active democratic participants in their educational communities. Although it would seem obvious that these schools would focus on student learning through critical analysis, many of the actual practices at these institutions do the opposite. After all, schools know that large lecture classes using multiple-choice exams are ineffective learning environments. We know that these schools know this because when they advertise their own Honors Colleges, they stress the fact that students learn in small seminars taught by expert professors who engage with students over their own ideas and writing.[1] Thus, while the privileged few are able to receive a high-quality education, many students are instructed in a low-quality system.

One possible result of large lecture classes is that students are socialized to just sit back and memorize fragmented bits of information.[2] These learners are not given the opportunity to interact with the knowledge in a creative and critical manner, and instead, they are told to internalize and retain what the expert says is important. The implicit lesson of these lectures is that people should simply listen to what the authority figure says, and there is no need for individual involvement or democratic participation. No wonder many students sleep in their lecture classes or surf the web or do not even attend—there really is no reason for them being present. The real question is why do colleges and universities allow this to go on? One reason is that universities believe that it costs much less to educate students in this way, and since no one is complaining, there is no reason to change things. Another factor is that it can be much easier for a professor to deliver a prepared lecture or PowerPoint presentation than to engage students in an active give and take. Also, some teachers do not want to spend a large amount of time grading papers, and so it is easier to give multiple-choice exams or have graduate students read student essays. No matter the explanation, students are often sent the message that their own schools and teachers do not care about providing an effective education.

If higher education is really about rationalizing social and economic inequality, then it does make sense not to stress student learning, but if we believe that school is about social and personal development, then the current system is highly ineffective. What is very concerning is the fact that at the same time students are receiving the message that learning does not really matter, they are also competing against each other for grades. As we saw in the last chapter, the effect of this type of social environment is that one learns to be a cynical conformist, which means one competes in a system in which one does not believe. From the perspective of social stability, cynical conformity may be the biggest benefit of our higher education system—our colleges and universities often train students to not care about the social systems around them; at the same time they are socialized to compete as isolated individuals for a scarce resource (grades).[3]

This critical perspective concerning the current state of higher education helps to explain why as our society has become more unequal and unjust, few educated people seem to get upset. The education system has unintentionally stumbled upon the best way to increase inequality and still retain social peace, and that is by socializing people to compete as individuals and not care about the surrounding social world. Yet if we do care about the future of our democracy and world, we need to rethink how students are taught, and this requires a major change in the priorities of higher education institutions.

Ranking the Rankings

Many critics have pointed out that even though universities criticize college ranking systems like *US News & World Report*, these institutions spend a great deal of time and money trying to increase their rankings.[4] Here, we see how cynical conformity starts at the top: although these schools know that these rankings do not examine the real quality of an institution, the schools conform to the priorities of the rankings in order to outcompete other schools. Thus, selective universities try to attract the students with the highest SAT scores, even though they know that SAT scores do not predict how well students will do in college.[5] Universities also increase their spending on research in order to increase their reputation as they downsize their instructional budgets since the quality of teaching or learning does not show up in the rankings. It is therefore not surprising that students also have internalized an attitude of cynical conformity since the leaders of their institutions have clearly embraced this type of psychology and political ideology.

It is important to stress that cynical conformity is a contradictory position because, on the one hand, it represents a loss of individuality by conforming to what others are doing, and, on the other hand, it enhances individualism through a competition of everyone against everyone else. According to the logic of the invisible hand, people acting as competing individuals contribute to the common good, but this free market myth is shown to be an illusion that helps to hide the destruction of the commons. In short, the invisible hand of capitalism is supposed to be the magic act that transforms individualistic competition into social sharing, and cynical conformity and the continued belief in the meritocracy help to cover the failure of the invisible hand to work its magic.

As inequality continues to grow and higher education continues to decrease and not enhance social mobility, the need to teach cynical conformity increases. Moreover, this attitude helps to solve the enduring American conflict between individualism and social cohesion: the best way to keep the ideology of individual liberty alive is to produce it through cynical conformity. Here, one can be both an isolated individual and conform to the group because one does not believe in one's own conformity.[6] We see this logic at play in universities competing in the rankings race and students competing for grades in classes that they do not care about. Moreover, although the faculty do not believe that they are teaching conformity, they often feel that they have no alternative but to lecture and use multiple-choice tests in large classes. What is being described here is an unintentional conspiracy: people on all levels are conforming to the system that produces cynical conformity in a cynical way.

The philosopher Slavoj Žižek has explained cynical conformity through the following story.[7] He relates that in the old Soviet Union, stores were constantly running out of goods, and so one day, a person went to the local store to buy toilet paper, and after making the purchase, he heard that the store had run out of this product. The shopper knew that there was toilet paper available because he saw it with his own eyes, but then he realized that if people think there is no toilet paper, they will go and buy it, and then there will really be no toilet paper; the original shopper then decides to go to the store and buy more paper to beat out the other shoppers. This story tells us that in the structure of cynical conformity, social logic can overcome individual experience. Thus, even though I see something with my own eyes, what matters more is what other people think. This logic applies to the stock market where people often buy or sell stocks based not on the perceived value of a company but what they think other people think the value is.

Within a market economy, where exchange value trumps use value, the value of something is determined by what people believe other people believe. In other words, it does not matter what I believe—it matters what others do. By removing social logic from personal belief and perception, conformity takes on a cynical edge: everyone is doing what they think everyone

TRAINING UNDEMOCRATIC CAPITALISTS   105

else will do, but no one necessarily believes in the truth of their own beliefs. Of course, one of the benefits of this system is that society does not have to force people to believe in anything, and individuals do not have to feel that they are responsible for their own actions. In fact, Descartes argued that social conformity allows people to escape from their own guilt, remorse, and vacillation through a displacement of responsibility.[8] However, this philosophy of cynical conformity is the opposite of critical thinking and the goals of democratic learning. If we want students to learn to think for themselves and critically examine knowledge and other social constructions, then we should not be teaching them how to conform from a position of distance.

Doing College

The education historian David Labaree has shown how the logic of cynical conformity may be the new guiding principle of the American education system. He posits that "doing school" means learning how to game the system from a position of distance.[9] In *How to Succeed in School Without Really Learning*, Labaree outlines the ways this educational mode of cynical conformity stems from the fact that education is supposed to be about both learning and social mobility.[10] However, these dual goals are often in conflict, and so the result can be a series of self-defeating compromises.

Labaree insists that instead of using schools as a place that helps private individuals get ahead, schools should have a public purpose. In other words, the stress on meritocracy creates a conflict between the private and the public that can only be resolved through a cynical combination of the two different agendas. In what is called the tragedy of the commons, when all the people pursue their own individual goals, the common good is undermined. For example, when farmers each increase their grazing in order to enhance their individual profits, they end up destroying the shared land.[11] Moreover, even if people are acting with the best of intentions, the summation of their actions can

106   TRAINING UNDEMOCRATIC CAPITALISTS

undermine their shared interests. In fact, a belief in the goodness of one's intentions may blind one from seeing the negative effects of one's actions.[12]

In terms of education, Labaree claims that the public good of providing socially useful learning is often undermined by the quest for individual credentials.[13] This contradiction also reflects on the fact that at the same time people are positioned to be consumers of education, they are also invested in the role education plays in promoting a more effective democracy and society.[14] Labaree adds that as parents and students see education as a system for personal advancement, the formal aspects of schooling—like grades, credentials, degrees—tend to dominate, and the signs of merit win out over actually learning.[15] In this structure, teaching becomes focused on sorting students and not instructing them; meanwhile, schools themselves have to compete in an open market for students. Ultimately, for Labaree the main question is a political one because it concerns what kind of schools we want, and this problem runs into the central conflict between democracy and capitalism.[16] Since total economic freedom leads to social inequality, but any attempt to create a more equal society results in a reduction of individual liberties, there is an unresolvable tension at the heart of modern American society.

In a later book, *Someone Has to Fail,* Labaree returns to this conflict between capitalistic individualism and democratic equality by arguing that in terms of K-12 schooling in America, the fact that all students are forced to go to school, but are also expected to develop an individual motivation to succeed, results in a situation where students "pretend to learn" by going "through the outward motions." This form of cynical conformity "is a compromise in which students acknowledge the teacher's control and the teacher uses this control lightly, making only modest demands on the students as learners."[17] In what is sometimes called the academic truce, the teachers and the students tacitly agree not to challenge each other, and thus the goal of teaching and learning critical thinking is surrendered.[18]

College Life against Critical Thinking

One place to examine how cynical conformity shapes higher education and undermines the quest to teach critical thinking can be found in ethnographic studies of college students' lives. In Rebekah Nathan's *My Freshman Year*, we see how students' perceptions and values are shaped by conflicting aspects of contemporary culture.[19] Her work shows that even though we are used to dividing college life into the two opposing spheres of class time and social time, the social aspects of education are constantly shaping the way students interact with their classes. Nathan argues that since students are free to choose as individuals their majors and their classes, a shared community can only be developed outside of class through sports and extracurricular activities. However, these social life aspects tend to crowd out the time that students have to focus on their education.[20] The end result of this battle between the social quest for fun and the educational quest for learning is that students take on a cynical attitude of equal anonymity into their classes. In other words, if they can attain a sense of invisibility in the classroom, they do not have to come prepared, and they will not be embarrassed in front of their fellow classmates.[21]

Nathan believes that there is a set of unconscious norms that regulates students' behaviors in the classroom. For example, students will signal to each other their dismay if another student participates too much or seems to be getting too close to the professor. In this form of cynical conformity, the students are unconsciously signaling to each other the need to stay "cool" and uninvolved or at the very least unenthusiastic. In fact, when Nathan interviewed students to see why they do not participate in class, she discovered that students often don't listen to each other, and they don't want to appear too smart or too stupid.[22] Students also complain that the teacher knows the right answer, so there is no reason for the teachers to try to get the students to come up with their own responses. Nathan concludes that peer pressure and a dependency on expert authority undermines

108   TRAINING UNDEMOCRATIC CAPITALISTS

student engagement and the school rhetoric of being a "free market place of ideas."[23] In short, she finds that universities often do not promote critical thinking or democratic participation, and the main reason for this is the way an unconscious peer culture dominates the classroom.

Nathan also noticed that when students left their classes, they rarely talked about the class content or any ideas; instead they discussed their social lives and what "work" they had to do for their classes.[24] Thus, as Labaree argues, students have been socialized to focus on the form and not the content of education, as they draw a strict boundary between their school life and their social life. Nathan adds that when she interviewed students about what they hope to get out of going to college, they stressed the idea that while they were in school to learn, most of what you learn is outside of classes and studying.[25] In fact, one student responded to a question of why she stays in school by stating that, "college is too fun. Granted, classes get in the way a bit but it's all worth the experience."[26]

Paying for Class

Some people may be turned off by what they see as a criticism of contemporary students, but it makes no sense to simply idealize students or ignore their attitudes toward higher education. Furthermore, as we see in Elizabeth Armstrong's and Laura Hamilton's *Paying for the Party*, the peer culture that affects the ability of students to think critically or engage in their classes also helps to reinforce negative social hierarchies and a tolerance for inequality. One of the key findings of Armstrong's and Hamilton's book is that as public universities seek to enroll more high-paying, out-of-state students to make up for reductions in state funding, these schools become dominated by a class-based, anti-intellectual social system.[27] In this dynamic, schools pour money into fancy dorms and extracurricular activities in order to attract wealthy students. One of the side effects of this competition for high-paying enrollments is that low-income students become disengaged from school and sometimes drop out because they cannot compete in the expensive, class-based social life. Here, economic inequality helps to determine who gets into college and how the college is changed in order to cater to affluent students. Moreover, once students graduate, the ones who come from wealth have a much easier time getting a job because they profit from their parents' social connections and family funds that support important internships in expensive cities.

Wrapped up in this class-based social hierarchy is a gender system that can push women to focus on their looks and not their studies. In fact, *Paying for the Party* documents how due to the power of sororities and fraternities in shaping the peer culture, female students often compete to get into the best clubs by having the most expensive clothing and "the best" bodies and faces. The Greek system is therefore one way that higher education can enhance and increase inequality as it shapes the values and beliefs of students. Moreover, some universities feed this system by creating "soft" majors and making it relatively easy for students to pass their classes with little effort.[28] Although public universities are supposed to fulfill a public mission, it is clear from this book that they often function to exaggerate class privilege and instill destructive social stereotypes. Meanwhile, students resist discussing issues like class, inequality, and sexual stereotypes in their classroom.

One would think that teachers would push past students' resistances to critical thinking, but teachers themselves are now forced to cater to students' desires because most of the faculty do not have tenure, and they are mostly hired and promoted based on student evaluations.[29] In other terms, teachers may have to please their students in the classroom, and this is done in part by giving them high grades and not challenging them too much. Likewise, some students seek to do as little work as possible so they can concentrate on their social lives. As Armstrong and Hamilton document, this stress on fun over learning has a long history in American higher education. In fact, the authors cite a president from Princeton from the early twentieth century who told the faculty that, "Gentlemen, whether we like it or not, we shall have to recognize that Princeton is a rich man's college and the rich men do not frequently come to college to study."[30] What has happened is that this upper-class notion that college is about socializing and building social networks has been democratized, and now many students from all classes believe that higher education is mostly about improving one's social life.

At the same time that going to school to party has spread throughout the class system, Armstrong and Hamilton document that partying itself is shaped by class hierarchies. For instance, they show that it is quite expensive to compete in the erotic marketplace and the Greek system because one must have enough money to buy expensive clothing, go on costly trips, pay for expensive outings, buy expensive cars, purchase costly beauty supplies, pay for clubs, and purchase drugs and alcohol.[31] In fact, one of their surprising findings is that non-wealthy students often drop out of school because they cannot afford to compete in the dominating high-cost social world.

Paying for the Party also documents how the college social life can function to sort students into groups that share the same class, race, and ethnic backgrounds.[32] Here, we see how institutions of higher education may unintentionally support the enhancement of inequality by refusing to interfere with the peer culture generated by the college social life system. Not only do schools do this by supporting the partying around athletic teams, but schools also cater to the Greek system by allowing them to purchase property and function on campus. Moreover, the authors of *Paying for the Party* suggest that sororities and fraternities are often the solution to the university issue of how to attract and keep students by maximizing the level of fun.[33] As Murray Sperber argued in *Beer and Circus*, many universities have discovered that it is much easier to satisfy students outside of class than inside, and so they pour money into supporting extracurricular activities. This process not only helps in attracting students whose families can pay the full cost of attending college, but it also feeds into the systematic undermining of critical thinking and student engagement in active learning.[34]

Although Armstrong and Hamilton describe how there are still students who strive to improve themselves in college by learning, these students appear to be the new minority on campus, and they have to work hard at resisting the temptations that are presented by the dominating peer culture. Also, the students who may most benefit from the class mobility that a university degree can offer are also the ones who are the most dependent on inadequate and inconsistent financial aid policies.[35] Furthermore, these students do not have the money to participate in the expensive peer culture, and so they often remove themselves from the main social life of the campus, and this makes them vulnerable to a sense of alienation, which can lead to dropping out or transferring to a local community college that does not have the same culture.

Armstrong and Hamilton found that the students who tend to profit the most from going to college are the ones who are on a professional track, and these are the wealthy students who enter the university with high grades and high SAT scores and are backed by professional parents who have a large amount of money to spend on study abroad programs and unpaid internships.[36] Here, the students who begin school and college with the biggest advantages also continue to profit from their parents' wealth and support; on the other hand, the students who do not have rich, supportive parents have a hard time affording the extra costs that help to build a student's resume and professional networks. The wealthier students are also the ones with the greatest ability to get the most out of the educational system since they have already had a long history of working the system and learning how to present themselves in a positive light to other members of elite institutions. Thus, just as K-12 schools place their students into different tracks, which have profound impacts on how students see themselves in the future, colleges and universities also track students in a much less obvious way.

Paying for the Party argues that while universities continue to signal their commitment to meritocracy and social mobility, the schools undermine these social goals by focusing on "prestige

112   TRAINING UNDEMOCRATIC CAPITALISTS

maximization" to recruit the highest-paying or most prepared students.[37] Once again, this quest to outcompete the other schools results in an institutional form of cynical conformity: all schools want to increase their prestige, even though they know that this competition undermines their ability to perform their central mission of educating students. As Armstrong and Hamilton note, universities have become reliant on wealthy students who do not need financial aid and do not demand much from their education.[38] However, the authors also indicate that this system cannot continue because the universities are running out of wealthy students who can fill their need, and so they are now turning to the global market for international students.[39] Of course, one of the unintended consequences of this dependency on high-paying, out-of-state, and international students is that in-state students are being shut out of their local public universities and colleges.

Drinking Not Thinking

As nonelite public universities seek to increase their share of high-paying students, they are unable to attract the most high-achieving ones, and so they have to settle for many students who have money but not a strong desire to learn. One of the only things that universities can do to help reverse the shift from partying to studying is to hold more classes on Friday and punish faculty for grade inflation, but schools have been for the most part unwilling to do this.[40] Schools could also increase the policing of student parties, but this strategy has also been resisted. Instead, institutions of higher education try to turn a blind eye to what happens outside of the classroom, and when a scandal or lawsuit occurs, they often focus on image and risk management.[41]

The failure of schools to confront the dominating social life has resulted in a growing outcry over sexual assault and an assortment of other campus crimes. In 2014, the federal government got involved when a group of female students issued a formal complaint over the way their schools handled their

TRAINING UNDEMOCRATIC CAPITALISTS 113

reports of sexual assault.[42] This situation has shown that universities and colleges are in a moral quandary: they do not want to alienate their students by cracking down on partying, but they also do not want to open themselves up to lawsuits and federal investigations.

As *Paying for the Party* documents, sexual assault is often fueled by binge drinking, and binge drinking is often promoted by fraternities and sororities.[43] Of course, college students have never needed an excuse to drink and have sex, but what has changed is the peer culture surrounding these activities. Many female students feel that they must drink to show themselves to be attractive to male students, and to overcome their conflicted feelings about being a sexual object, they drink so they do not have to think. Likewise, the men often drink to overcome their own inhibitions and moral uneasiness, and the result can be that in an institution dedicated to thinking, people are doing anything they can do not to think about the consequences of their actions.

Armstrong and Hamilton also indicate that one change in the current culture is that women now compete with each other by displaying their "sexual prowess."[44] Furthermore, since many women do not go to college to find someone to marry as they did in the past, females are much freer to experiment with their sexuality. In this culture, some women determine their place in the social hierarchy by hooking up with a male who has a certain status in the eyes of the peer group. Here, we see how inequality is maintained and enhanced through the social sorting mechanism that couples people from similar class and race backgrounds.

This implicit peer culture is also affected by a new type of "feminism," which defines a female's power and freedom through her ability to be sexually desirable.[45] In the logic of empowerment through consented subordination, many young women trick themselves into believing that they have total control over their sexual relationships. This new form of feminism has been developed at a time when a record number of women are going to and graduating from college, and thus it is important to examine

114 TRAINING UNDEMOCRATIC CAPITALISTS

how the combination of self-empowerment and a submission to a traditional gender hierarchy helps to reinforce inequality in higher education.

Joining Exclusivity

Greek systems also function as selective clubs within already selective higher education institutions. This point is made clearly and repetitively in the film *The Social Network*. Although the film is about Mark Zuckerberg's creation of Facebook, the story is centered on an attempt to create exclusivity at an institution that is already highly exclusive. According to the movie, Zuckerberg wanted to produce a selective site that would only cater to students from Harvard. In fact, the first part of the film alternates between scenes depicting the partying going on at a Harvard Final Club (fraternity) with scenes of Zuckerberg building and circulating his own online site that rates Harvard women one against the other. Furthermore, the movie opens with a dialogue between Zuckerberg and his soon-to-be former girlfriend, and the main topic is his desire to get into a highly exclusive club. After Zuckerberg tells her that if he gets into the club, he will be able to bring her to parties and introduce her to a new class of people, his girlfriend, who goes to a less prestigious college, becomes enraged and breaks up with him. In response to the breakup, he writes a horrible blog entry mocking her looks, and then he decides to use the Harvard directories (Facebook) that are attached to every dorm to compare and rank Harvard women. One of the world's largest businesses and virtual hubs is thus depicted as originating from sexual rejection and a desire to join a highly exclusive club.

The narrative of this film tells us much about contemporary culture, inequality, higher education, and the resistance to critical thinking. In the constant attempt to climb up the social hierarchy, people demand more and more selectivity and exclusiveness, and just as colleges are ranked in part by how many students they reject, the push for increased social status for some means that many people will be excluded. Furthermore, as

TRAINING UNDEMOCRATIC CAPITALISTS 115

women become the dominant population in higher education, they have been motivated to buy into a peer and media culture that devalues them and sells submission as a sign of strength. Making matters worse, instead of college and university educators being able to confront and possibly resist these aspects of destructive social inequality, the faculty without tenure are now subjected to reductive student evaluations, which makes the teachers themselves subject to adolescent peer culture.

In another layer of cynical conformity, administrators know that student evaluations are not effective tools for assessing faculty, but they rely on these forms because they are so easy to process and utilize. Of course, the fear of getting a bad student evaluation will influence a faculty member who does not have tenure, and so even if the teacher believes that his or her students are not thinking in a critical manner or participating in class activities, the teacher may still reward the students with high grades just to keep his or her job. On the other hand, some professors with tenure often have no real incentive to teach in an effective manner or motivate their students because they are hired and promoted based on their research and not their teaching. Therefore, it is just a myth to say that institutions of higher education teach critical thinking and democratic participation; rather, what they most often teach is cynical conformity, and this cannot be a good thing for individuals or society.

Notes

1 Sperber, Murray. *Beer and circus: How big-time college sports has crippled undergraduate education.* Macmillan, 2000: x.
2 Samuels, Robert. *Why public higher education should be free: How to decrease cost and increase quality at American universities.* Rutgers University Press, 2013: 29–25.
3 Sloterdijk, Peter. *Critique of cynical reason.* Minneapolis: University of Minnesota Press, 1987.
4 Silverman, Jacob. "How college rankings work." http://money.howstuff works.com/personal-finance/college-planning/admissions/college-ranking2.htm.
5 Fairtest. "SAT I: A faulty instrument for predicting college success." http://fairtest.org/sat-i-faulty-instrument-predicting-college-success.

TRAINING UNDEMOCRATIC CAPITALISTS

6 In the film *The matrix*, Morpheus tells Neo that he has the look of a man who accepts what he sees because he expects to wake up.

7 Žižek, Slavoj. "The object as a limit of discourse: Approaches to the lacanian real*." *Prose Studies* 11.3 (1988): 94–120.

8 Descartes, René. *Discourse on method, optics, geometry, and meteorology.* Hackett Publishing, 2001.

9 Labaree, David F. *Someone has to fail.* Harvard University Press, 2012: 219.

10 Labaree, David F. *How to succeed in school without really learning: The credentials race in American education.* Yale University Press, 1997: 1.

11 This is called the tragedy of the commons. See "The Tragedy of the Commons." *Science* 162 (3859): 1243–1248. 1968. doi:10.1126/science. 162.3859.1243.

12 Stannard-Stockton, Sean. "Good intentions vs. good results." www. tacticalphilanthropy.com/2011/04/good-intentions-vs-good-results/.

13 Labaree, *How*: 2.

14 Ibid.

15 Ibid.

16 Ibid., 16.

17 Labaree, *Someone:* 139.

18 Sperber, 13.

19 Nathan, Rebekah. "My freshman year." *Perspectives: Teaching legal research and writing* 14.3 (2006); Armstrong, Elizabeth A. *Paying for the party.* Harvard University Press, 2013.

20 Nathan, 42.

21 Ibid., 19.

22 Ibid., 94.

23 Ibid., 95.

24 Ibid., 96.

25 Ibid., 101.

26 Ibid., 102.

27 Armstrong and Hamilton, 8.

28 Ibid., 16.

29 Benjamin, Ernst. "How over-reliance on contingent appointments diminishes faculty involvement in student learning." *Change* 1995.1975 (1975): 1995; Langen, Jill M. "Evaluation of adjunct faculty in higher education institutions." *Assessment & Evaluation in Higher Education* 36.2 (2011): 185–196; Cross, John G., and Edie N. Goldenberg. "How does university decision making shape the faculty?." *New Directions for Higher Education* 2003.123 (2003): 49–59.

30 Armstrong, 11.

31 Ibid., 11.

32 Ibid., 10.

33 Ibid., 15.

34 Sperber.

35 Armstrong, 17.

TRAINING UNDEMOCRATIC CAPITALISTS 117

36 Ibid., 19.
37 Ibid., 20.
38 Ibid., 21.
39 Ibid., 31.
40 Toomey, Traci L.., and Alexander C. Wagenaar. "Environmental policies to reduce college drinking: Options and research findings." *Journal of Studies on Alcohol and Drugs* 14 (2002): 193.
41 The Penn State sexual abuse scandal is a good example of a school focusing its attention on image control instead of dealing with the problem.
42 CBS News. "Federal government names 55 colleges facing sexual assault investigations." www.cbsnews.com/news/federal-government-names-55-colleges-facing-sexual-assault-investigations/.
43 Wechsler, Henry, et al. "Trends in college binge drinking during a period of increased prevention efforts: Findings from 4 Harvard School of Public Health College Alcohol Study surveys: 1993–2001." *Journal of American College Health* 50.5 (2002): 203–217.
44 Armstrong, 87.
45 Levy, Ariel. *Female chauvinist pigs: Women and the rise of raunch culture.* Simon and Schuster, 2006.

7

THE DEATH OF THE LIBERAL CLASSROOM

Since the mid-1970s, universities have been attacked by conservatives for being bastions of Left-wing indoctrination.[1] However, we have already seen that these schools are actually quite conservative, and if anything, they often feed into a social hierarchy that does not promote critical thinking or democratic student engagement. So, the question remains of why this myth about the liberal nature of these institutions still continues, and how does it reflect on the politics of inequality? Of course, one of the key reasons why conservatives like to call these institutions liberal is that it helps to create a clear enemy, which aids in the effort of keeping the conservative coalition together. Since the 1970s, one of the only things unifying Christian fundamentalists, libertarians, nationalists, and business interests is a shared dislike for liberals and their institutions. In one of the greatest public relations manipulations of all time, conservative think tanks, pundits, and politicians have been able to convince themselves and the general public that the real elites in our society are the liberal media, universities, and political officials.[2] According to this myth, the center of power that generates inequality, then, is not wealthy people and big businesses; instead, the liberal elite controls the culture and the economy.

The irony is that as the conservative attack on universities increased after 1980, these institutions continued to become more conservative in their practices. Moreover, as states decreased their funding for universities and colleges, and these schools had to become more entrepreneurial, the same institutions were

THE DEATH OF THE LIBERAL CLASSROOM 119

criticized for being anticapitalist.[3] Thus, part of the reason why we still think that higher education institutions are the last bastion of liberalism is because the conservative media continue to repeat this message. However, we shall see that these schools actually consider themselves to be liberal institutions, and so we must return to the original question of how a conservative institution maintains a liberal reputation.

Values vs. Actions

First of all, many professors do tend to vote as moderates or Democrats, and so it is true that they do hold progressive values and beliefs; the problem is that once they enter into their jobs, they often do not act in a liberal or progressive fashion.[4] After all, it is hard to imagine how anyone who really believed in liberal causes would support the type of labor hierarchy that we see in higher education today. Furthermore, the admission policies of many of these "liberal" institutions are anything but liberal.[5] Although many school officials talk a great deal about diversity and equal opportunity, their policies often enhance inequality. Likewise, many faculty teach about democracy and critical thinking as they lecture to a silent group of memorizing students. In the case of both liberal administrators and professors, their words simply do not often match their actions.

One of the clearest ways to show the lack of liberalism in higher education is to examine the effect of the divide between tenured professors and nontenure-track faculty. Although professors argue that tenure is needed to protect academic freedom, they do not usually act to change a system where most of the faculty lack tenure or academic freedom.[6] Professors also argue that they need tenure to protect their role in shared governance, but these same professors allow most of the faculty to be excluded from the right to participate in their own departments or faculty senates.[7] Meanwhile, as professors complain about the loss of public funding for higher education, many support a star system that allows some professors to renegotiate higher salaries and lower course loads.[8] Likewise, professors often argue

120 THE DEATH OF THE LIBERAL CLASSROOM

for more graduate students to take their graduate seminars and teach their undergraduate courses even though they know these doctoral students have a very low chance of getting a tenure-track job once they graduate. None of these actions by professors could be called liberal or progressive, and yet the myth remains that these institutions are run by liberal elites.

Of course, conservative politicians and pundits like to attack colleges and universities for being liberal because they want to justify cutting the public support for these institutions as they explain how students are being indoctrinated by Left-wing professors.[9] The irony of this situation is that from a conservative perspective, the best place for radical activists is in a university or college because that means they are not in the streets threatening the social order. However, some conservatives still believe in the myth that university professors are training their students to be liberals or progressives.[10] Yet, as I discussed in the previous chapters, higher education institutions are often socializing students to be cynical conformists, which can only help the conservative cause.

Even if students did simply copy what their liberal professors say and molded their beliefs to match the progressive beliefs of their teachers, it turns out that many liberals not only act like conservatives, but they also have bought into a conservative ideology. After all, many professors are obsessed about rankings, ratings, and prestige, and departments and professors often want to hire the next star from a prestigious Ivy League school, while they ignore the fact that most of their students are being taught by underpaid, part-time faculty.[11]

Institutional Suicide

Chris Hedges' *The Death of the Liberal Class* helps us to understand how and why the liberal university has been transformed into a system of exploitation and undemocratic competition.[12] Hedges argues that all of our major liberal institutions (universities, unions, the Democratic Party, journalism, and the arts) have been taken over by individuals whose main concern is protecting

THE DEATH OF THE LIBERAL CLASSROOM 121

their own careers. From this perspective, liberal professors undermine the public good by using public institutions to promote their own private wealth and prestige. Moreover, according to Hedges, in order to protect the status quo that has made them successful, liberal professionals demonize any radical alternative that would make society more just and fair.

We can relate Hedges' interpretation to Robert Nisbet's 1971 book *The Degradation of Academic Dogma.*[13] Nisbet argues that after World War II, federal funding poured into American universities to do military and scientific research, and when research professors realized that they could increase their pay and prestige by focusing on funded research, they turned their teaching duties over to graduate students and part-time faculty. One of the results of this transformation of higher education was that research was valued over teaching and the sciences become more privileged than the humanities. According to this narrative, the source, then, for the neglect of undergraduate education was not the defunding of public universities or the priorities of business-oriented administrators; rather, the combination of increased governmental funding and professorial greed resulted in a new form of academic capitalism. Liberal universities were then undermined mostly from within when liberal professors transformed public institutions through a focus on private rewards.

Nisbet's theory directly conflicts with the dominant narrative that liberals like to tell about their own institutions. Instead of universities being ruined by conservative ideologies and cost-cutting states and administrators, an internal process of professional careerism transformed these institutions from the inside. Therefore, instead of blaming the external political and cultural system for the problems now plaguing higher education, we should first look at how the destructive reward systems and hierarchies were generated from within the liberal institutions themselves. In other words, it was the individualistic quest for prestige and more compensation that may have turned these last bastions of liberalism into neoliberal institutions.

122   THE DEATH OF THE LIBERAL CLASSROOM

It has been my experience that liberal professors hate this explanation because they would rather believe that they are blameless and do not participate in generating inequality and downgrading educational quality. It is much easier and comforting to blame clueless administrators or evil politicians for defunding higher education, and while it is true that state cuts in higher education support have played an important role in downsizing the missions of these schools and increasing tuition, it is important to look at the internal reasons for educational inequality and academic labor exploitation. Meanwhile, as tenure becomes the privileged protection of a dwindling number of faculty, we have to ask why the protected professors have not done more to fight the negative trends that have reshaped their institutions. In other words, why have the tenured professors not fought for equal rights for all faculty and a stronger commitment to undergraduate education and a more fair and equal admissions system?

It turns out that the liberal professors have often ignored inequality and exploitation because their jobs depend on not challenging the status quo. Instead of organizing together to make higher education more just and equal, the liberal professors have tended to double down on the myths of the fair meritocracy. To justify their own relative privilege, many promote a rhetoric of diversity and opportunity as they cash in on a system of inequality and labor exploitation. Thus, the same faculty who work with exploited part-time, insecure faculty argue that we need more graduate students to be trained for academic jobs that no longer exist, and as the size of ineffective undergraduate lecture classes continues to expand, the professors fight for more resources to go into research and graduate education.

The moral hypocrisy of the liberal class and the neoliberal classroom can be revealed by looking at how progressive professors often describe the causes for the changes in higher education. For instance, in *Neoliberalism's Attack on Higher Education*, Henry Giroux states that democracy can only flourish if people learn how to connect their private problems to larger public

THE DEATH OF THE LIBERAL CLASSROOM   123

issues.[14] However, a problem with his analysis is that he sees this blockage of critical dialogue in higher education as coming from a "Right-wing war" on critical literacy, while I have been showing how many of the destructive practices of higher education come primarily from "liberal" professors within "liberal" institutions.[15] In fact, one way that Giroux and other Left-wing critics focus their attention on external forces is through the notion that "corporate management models" have pushed schools to replace full-time, tenured faculty with part-time, nontenure-track faculty.[16] The problem with this analysis is that it has often been professors who have directly created and maintained this system of labor inequality. Like the problem with grading, it is hard to see how the use and abuse of contingent faculty will change if the professors themselves do not realize the role they play in instituting regimes of inequality. Of course, it is much more satisfying to blame external forces for internal problems, but the faculty have to understand how they have bought into the combination of modern capitalism and science in the pursuit for higher rankings, ratings, and salaries.

As Giroux himself notes, "Critical thinking divorced from action is often as sterile as actions divorced from critical theory."[17] The problem with this statement is that many of the most prominent promoters of critical theory are not critical of the system that allows some people to do theory as most others have low-paid, non-research, part-time teaching positions. Moreover, although his book is focused on what he calls critical pedagogy (teaching), there are virtually no references to actual classroom practices in his book. In other words, the theory of critical teaching is detached from the messy work of dealing with actual students and the internal culture of grading and testing.

To be fair to Giroux, he is one of the only academic theory stars to examine the problems facing the exploitation of academic labor, yet the power of his critique is undermined by his need to shift the blame and attention to "the broader authoritarian forces now threatening the United States."[18] This overgeneralized rhetoric blinds him from seeing how Darwinian

124 THE DEATH OF THE LIBERAL CLASSROOM

capitalism is tied to the internal belief in the meritocracy and the need to grade and judge everything. For example, in the following passage, we see how education is positioned as a passive victim of a neoliberal attack:

> At the level of higher education, the script is similar with a project to defund higher education, impose corporate models of governance, purge the university of critical thinkers, turn faculty into a low-wage army of part-time workers, and allow corporate money and power to increasingly decide course content and determine what faculty get hired.[19]

In contrast to Giroux, I have been arguing that faculty at universities and colleges have directly contributed to many of the policies that Giroux blames on the corporate takeover of higher ed.

One explanation for this need to blame others is that liberals often want to see themselves as all good, and so they have a hard time admitting that they are part of the problem. For example, the same professors who often criticize the loss of tenure for most faculty continue to fight for more graduate students so that they can have students to take their graduate seminars and teach their undergraduate courses. Furthermore, the critique of higher education has rarely touched on the questions of grading, which represent one of the key ways that education is shaped by a capitalist ethos.

While Giroux states that he wants to promote a mode of teaching that teaches students through dialogue about the importance of power and social responsibility, his failure to take on the issue of grading prevents his theory from fully dealing with the reality of teaching in higher education today.[20] Even if a teacher wants to present a progressive class content through a discussion-based system, it does not mean that students will no longer be influenced by the power of the teacher to ration out rewards (grades). To challenge the power of teachers in the classroom without also challenging the role played by grading is like critiquing capitalism without dealing with capital.[21]

THE DEATH OF THE LIBERAL CLASSROOM   125

Giroux's critique reveals an interesting aspect concerning America's Left: while it is very effective at criticizing the ideology and policies on the Right, it has a hard time proposing any alternatives because everyone is so compromised by the capitalism of their everyday life.[22] As I have been arguing by analyzing the role of grades, rankings, and ratings in higher education, we see how the logic and ideology of capitalism now structures many aspects of our lives that are not directly economic. Furthermore, through the theory of cynical conformity, we see that even if individuals do not believe in the underlying ideology supporting their actions, they can still conform to the dominant belief system.

One place where we see this liberal problem of staying pure by blaming others is in Giroux's claim that popular culture is what teaches students to celebrate unbridled individualism and disdain community, public values, and the public good.[23] The problem with this analysis is that universities and K-12 schools also train students and faculty to celebrate individualism as they ignore the common good. Moreover, since liberals have not been able to pose a viable alternative to the extension of the market into all aspects of human existence, they are caught in a situation where they must critique the systems that they perpetuate on a daily basis. This type of self-contradiction not only leads to cynical conformity, but it also caters to an ironic mind-set where one critiques society from a position of individual innocence. Like the use of "scare quotes," liberal irony and humor are centered on a divided self and a doubled discourse that can only critique what it is about to repeat.[24] Irony then allows people the ability to maintain two opposing positions on the same topic. In the case of higher education, some liberal professors critique the way the system has been taken over by capitalism, but they do not want to see how their own practices contribute to this problem.[25]

The related problem with grading and ranking everything is that it immediately creates a hierarchy and a system of individual rewards that goes against the desires of liberal teachers to have

126   THE DEATH OF THE LIBERAL CLASSROOM

a more equal and sharing culture. Likewise, antiauthoritarian faculty do not want to be placed in a position of power, and yet their perceived need to give grades forces them to maintain an oppressive educational hierarchy. One of the effects of this internal conflict haunting liberal professors is that they have to deny their part in reproducing inequality as they conform to practices that produce unequal outcomes. For example, Giroux argues that all faculty have to "unsettle and oppose all orthodoxies," but he does not provide a way for teachers to remove themselves from the power of grading.[26] Moreover, the inability of critics like Giroux to provide alternatives to grading, student evaluations, large lecture classes, and multiple-choice tests prevents them from taking a strong stance against what they see as "the cult of measurement and efficiencies."[27]

Conservative Science

This implicit undemocratic investment in educational capitalism is supported by the emergence of several new fields that all tend to rationalize our unequal social systems. The recent areas gaining the most support and attention are neuroscience, evolutionary psychology, and behavioral economics, and although some people in these fields think they are liberal, the underlying message is often that we are all biologically programmed by evolution to automatically and unconsciously support the social hierarchy. Moreover, these disciplines tend to teach students and the general public that we can do little to change human nature, and so most progressive public policies or educational efforts will fail in the face of inherited biological mental programs. In other words, we are born to compete for scarce resources and protect and replicate our genetic material, which entails protecting people who look like us and avoiding people who look differently. This new form of social Darwinism has been enhanced through the use of expensive new technologies that supposedly map the brain and let us see how most of our thoughts and actions are unconscious and driven by evolution.[28]

THE DEATH OF THE LIBERAL CLASSROOM   127

John Tooby, one of the founders of evolutionary psychology, has compared the human brain to an iPhone full of different apps.[29] His argument is that evolution has selected certain mental programs because they help to solve discrete human problems like finding a suitable mate or detecting who is cheating the social group. These inherited biological programs are mostly unconscious and intuitive, and since they are derived from evolution, they are also universal. In other words, while we think that we are shaped by culture and our surrounding environment, evolutionary psychologists believe that we are preprogramed by nature, and since it takes a very long time for natural selection to shape our genetic material, these scientists affirm that our brains are running on old and outdated software.[30] The ultimate ideology that is produced by this return to social Darwinism is a conservative effort in naturalizing the status quo. Thus, my argument is that far from supporting a liberal ideology, many universities today are unknowingly helping to produce and circulate a new conservative version of social Darwinism that helps to rationalize inequality and naturalize capitalistic competition.

The Computer Brain

The metaphor of seeing our brains as computers or iPhones is also prevalent in neuroscience, where recent research shows how most of our mental process are not conscious; in fact, like evolutionary psychologists, neuroscientists tend to see the mind as determined by specific inherited biological structures, and these structures or programs can be localized using new brain imaging technologies such as fMRIs, which tie a specific mental function to a specific part of the brain; these functions are, in turn, connected to specialized neurotransmitters.[31] In this new mapping of the mind, computer scientists and cognitive scientists often translate neural networks into language processing machines.[32]

By seeing the human mind as a computer or iPhone, it becomes apparent that we are preprogramed by nature to perform

128 THE DEATH OF THE LIBERAL CLASSROOM

certain mental tasks in a quick and automatic fashion, and yet, I will argue that this entire theory is in actuality a political philosophy dressed in the rhetoric of science. The first move in this rhetorical construction of science is to equate the mind with the brain, and therefore, the difference between thinking and processing information is erased. This move is followed by the idea that any mental process that is unconscious or automatic must be by definition universal and biological. Here, two goals are accomplished at once: the unconscious is removed from culture and history and the role of human intention and free will is greatly reduced. Moreover, years of social science research are erased by arguing that any social mental function, which is superfast and nonconscious, must have been inherited from natural selection, and therefore its origins predate modern culture and current social influences.[33] These rhetorical moves have tremendous political and educational implications.

The Politics of Brain Science

A good understanding of the underlying politics of these new sciences can be gained by looking at an evolutionary psychology study purporting to show that the reason why some people do not like social welfare programs is that we have inherited a biological app that helps us to detect cheaters.[34] The way that this evolutionary software is tested is that people are given a survey online, and if they answer very quickly to particular questions, it is assumed that their responses are unconscious, automatic, and thus, biological.[35] These findings are then reversed, engineered, and projected back onto the hunter-gatherer period, which evolutionary psychologists believe was dominated by a social environment of scarcity and uncertain resources.[36] According to this logic, since the people in the hunter-gatherer society never knew when they would find their next prey, they needed to save their food and make sure that no one took too much. The next move in this theory is to argue that when people today think about welfare programs, they utilize their inherited cheater-detector programs, and thus they base their support or rejection of welfare

THE DEATH OF THE LIBERAL CLASSROOM   129

on their perceptions of whether the recipients of governmental programs are cheating the group.

Underlying this entire theory is a logic of scarcity and a need to detect social cheaters—whether they are constructed as being "Welfare Queens" or "illegal immigrants." Moreover, the theoretical foundation of neuroscience and evolutionary psychology tends to support the notion that we are preprogramed by our genes, and our genes are controlled by natural selection, and therefore it is hard to have any real type of education or social intervention. This is also a new form of social Darwinism: neuroscience and evolutionary psychology often reinforce the idea that our abilities and mental functions are inherited, and thus our social hierarchies and inequalities are natural and inevitable.[37]

Although some neuroscientists do stress the fact that brains can change over time (neuroplasticity) and the effect of current environment on our genes (epigenesis), books like Steven Pinker's *The Blank Slate* emphasize that our minds are dominated by inherited universal biological structures.[38] In fact, at the end of his book, Pinker lists over two hundred of these evolutionary universals, and they range from aesthetics to weapons.[39] From this perspective, contemporary culture is mostly window dressing covering our preprogrammed intuitions. Yet, even though Pinker rejects the value and effect of culture and political intervention, he spends most of his book attacking social science and liberal political policies. In other words, at the same time that he argues biology trumps culture, he obsesses over how liberal culture has miseducated our society. Like the conservatives who continue to attack universities for being liberal when these institutions have become more conservative, Pinker and other evolutionary psychologists critique the liberal social sciences even though these "natural" scientists do not believe that these soft sciences have any value or effect on people.

Pinker's attacks on feminism, the welfare state, anti-prejudice education, and progressive parenting techniques feed a conservative libertarian ideology, which has as its central premise the idea that we cannot change people's minds or their lives through

130   THE DEATH OF THE LIBERAL CLASSROOM

education or social welfare programs because people function largely in an intuitive and irrational way. Thus, any conscious attempt to regulate markets or redistribute income will fail; moreover, the unregulated free market mimics natural selection by automatically determining the winners and the losers in a distributed and unconscious way. Interestingly, one of the greatest heroes of this libertarian ideology is the economist F.A. Hayek, who argued that governmental policies often lead to serfdom because no single individual can understand the totality of an economic and social system.[40] Furthermore, Hayek saw free markets as affirmations of Adam Smith's idea that people acting selfishly will contribute to the common good, and thus prices are stabilized by a bottom-up process where individual demands meet the appropriate supply.

The Libertarian Web

Hayek's economic model should remind us of the ideology of the Web and the notion that everyone in the hive knows a little, and by combining our knowledge, we can come up with something like Wikipedia, which is a social network of information. For example, in an experiment based on this principle of the wisdom of the crowd, a professor places a glass jar of jellybeans in front of a class of undergraduate students and asks each student to guess the number of beans. The professor then shows that while no one guessed the exact number, the average of all of the guesses is very close to the truth. The lesson here is that individually we are dumb, but together we are smart.[41] However, as I have argued, this theory of the wisdom of the crowds can also be connected to the tragedy of the commons and the mythic investment in the invisible hand of the free market.

Many progressive educators have been seduced by this notion of collective or distributed intelligence, and we shall see that it fits well with evolutionary psychology's metaphor of Darwin's iPhone and our current political order. From a libertarian perspective, the ultimate value is individual liberty, which is often understood as the right of individuals and corporations to trade

THE DEATH OF THE LIBERAL CLASSROOM 131

freely with each other.[42] In this model of society, we are all isolated individuals plugged into particular social networks and markets that serve to select winners and losers in an ongoing natural experiment. Like the popular investment in reality television, competitive games, and social rankings, we spend our time monitoring structures of unnatural selection. For instance, in the case of Reality TV, real people often compete for a scarce resource as members are voted off the island or judged to not make the next round.[43] In terms of education, standardized tests rate and rank students and schools in order to select who will survive and who will fail. Here, education becomes a competitive game based not on learning but rather based on earning (grades, credits, degrees). Moreover, universities compete with each other for students and prestige, while faculty compete for grants to do research. From this perspective, higher education has become marketized, and the old separation between science and capitalism has been lost. In other terms, while people still think of university science as being objective, neutral, and universal, this objectivity becomes diluted if it is shaped by larger market forces, and as I have been arguing throughout this chapter, the end result of this new form of social Darwinism is that the progressive meritocracy is transformed into the ideology of the libertarian invisible hand. Thus, universities may still talk the language of liberalism, and they may still be full of liberal professors, but they function to rationalize inequality and the status quo.

Education, the Web, and New Social Darwinism

Kathy Davidson's book *Now You See It* brings together many of the themes discussed above. She believes, like many educational technology enthusiasts, that we need to turn education into gaming and replace lectures and books with online projects and problem-solving activities.[44] In her conception of the human mind, she argues that we now live in a multitasking culture that does not reward sustained attention on a single task, and our students are often bored after only a few minutes of reading or listening. Moreover, using a model of intelligence derived in part from Hayek, she posits that since we all have very limited perspectives, we must learn how to crowdsource our knowledge, and thus education should be based on collaboration.[45]

Davidson insists that since focus and attention blind us from seeing things outside of our limited view, we should restructure higher education so that knowledge is collected and shared. Although this seems like a well-intentioned, progressive idea, the problem is that it feeds into the downsizing of faculty expertise and a naturalization of capitalistic logic. In other words, the new idea that students should teach and grade each other helps to usher in an educational system where professors are so devalued that they no longer have to be paid a living wage. As we see throughout the new Web-based economy, many of the new jobs are voluntary or very low paid, and although the ethic of free sharing can be applauded, it has darker implications for labor and inequality.[46]

One can argue that sites like Facebook, Wikipedia, and *The Huffington Post* represent a new model of high-tech capitalism based on the idea that most of the labor is done for free and voluntarily. In other words, people go on Facebook and post information and publish consumer preferences, which is then sold for a profit by the owners of the site. Likewise, individuals write content for *The Huffington Post*, but most of them are not paid, and when the company was sold, most of the writers did not share in the profits. The unintended side effect of creating a bottom-up culture of distributed knowledge is that the knowledge creators are often not compensated.[47] In fact, American universities have been innovators in creating new forms of free and just-in-time labor through their use of internships, contingent faculty, graduate student instructors, peer teachers, and student-led teaching.

The logic behind this new "liberal" system of inequality and unemployment draws equally from free market libertarianism and a reductive understanding of natural selection. From the perspective of libertarian ideology, systems work best when there is no regulation or planning because the planners never have

THE DEATH OF THE LIBERAL CLASSROOM 133

enough knowledge to make good decisions. Moreover, this promotion of free market fundamentalism is combined with the Darwinian idea that evolution does not follow any intentional plan; instead, particular traits survive in particular environments, and this means they have been selected in an unplanned, natural way. When natural selection is combined with free markets, the result is that markets are naturalized and nature itself becomes marketized. To be precise, the political message is that it is natural and thus inevitable to have free markets, and nature itself functions like a market economy.

In an interesting combination of libertarian economics, evolutionary theory, and neuroscience, Davidson argues that "an infant's brain matures by selection."[48] She makes this claim by combining the neuroscientific idea that as our brains develop, unneeded and unused neurons are pruned with the notion that our attention is always based on a selected focus. Here, natural selection is being confused with cognitive selection in order to bathe her educational theory in the authority of science and naturalized inevitability. While it is clear that Davidson believes that she is a progressive, underlying her interpretation is a belief in the libertarian free market, which is applied to all aspects of the human mind and higher education.

A key ideological trick of libertarian thinking is to remove the public realm from the relation between isolated individuals and networked markets. Thus, just as the individual capitalist is supposed to contribute to the common good by acting in a selfish way, free market enthusiasts argue that if we remove government regulation and planning, supply and demand will create a perfect system of self-regulation. The new twist on this theory is that the Web helps to provide the information that is needed so that buyers and producers can make their trades based on self-interested rationality.[49] Of course, after the Financial Meltdown of 2008, even former Federal Reserve Chair Alan Greenspan, a devotee of the libertarian Ayn Rand, declared that there was a flaw in his theory that the markets would be able to regulate themselves.[50]

134   THE DEATH OF THE LIBERAL CLASSROOM

Drawing on the self-regulation of markets and the self-direction of young people on the Web, Davidson argues that we should reshape education to match the decentralized, bottom-up logic of contemporary culture.[51] Like the proponents of anarchistic social movements (think Occupy Wall Street) and non-hierarchical businesses (think Valve Corporation), the idea here is that we no longer need managers or hierarchies, and the best types of systems are totally democratic ones like Wikipedia where anyone can participate in an open structure. Yet, there are several problems with these utopian social systems. First, they tend to retain but hide more traditional hierarchies under the cover of being totally open and democratic. Second, they render decision making very difficult, and they also do not allow for much planning or sustained organization.[52] Third, they tend to discount the role played by expertise, which can also mean the role played by education. In fact, Davidson states that "the fundamental principle of all crowdsourcing is that difference and diversity—not expertise and uniformity—solve problems."[53] In this false opposition, she places expertise on one side along with uniformity and difference and diversity on the other side. Yet, this is an unfair distinction because expertise does not require uniformity, and there is not a strict opposition between diversity and expertise. What this model does is to downgrade the need for expert professors and the entire system that funds and supports Davidson's own research and teaching.

In fact, one of Davidson's most radical ideas is to remove expertise and hierarchy from her class by letting students grade each other's work.[54] Once again, this sounds like a very progressive idea, but it ignores that this system turns the students into free laborers: in other terms, they end up doing the work for the teacher, but they are not paid, and at the same time, the rationale for paying the professor is also undermined. Like so many other progressive educational strategies, the problem is that education is removed from considerations concerning labor, economic value, and existing social hierarchies.

THE DEATH OF THE LIBERAL CLASSROOM   135

Like many other liberal high-tech evangelists, some of Davidson's educational innovations are inspired by an idealization of virtual reality: "Money, time, space, danger, skills, and difference can be overcome by the affordances of virtual worlds."[55] In response to this idealization of gaming and virtual educational settings, we have to ask whether we want to remove things like time, space, and difference from our learning environments. Moreover, this representation of an idealized virtual learning experience points to another flaw in the libertarian free market ideology; what is often missing in the representation of open markets is the role played by conflict, tension, irrationality, and shared social commitment. Also, in the integrated circuits of isolated individuals hooked up to the same network or market, the role played by social mediation is most often hidden from view.

Invasion of the Massive Open Online Course

Many of Davidson's ideas have made their way into the latest education craze: MOOCs (massive open online courses). Online providers like Coursera and Udacity claim that thousands of students can be given a superior education for virtually no cost through the magic of distance education. At the heart of their project is the idea that huge online classes can be made personal through the use of computer grading and student crowdsourcing.[56] Promoters of MOOCs also proclaim that by getting rid of the traditional lecture and textbook, students can be instantly tested on how well they do on specific tasks or quizzes. Borrowing from evolutionary psychology, the new online providers see the student as an iPhone with separate apps responding to specific tasks; some of these tasks are presented in games or challenges, while other tasks are collaborative and crowdsourced.[57] Yet, what is missing from this type of education is any idea of a student as a complete person with a single consciousness. In short, while evolutionary psychologists, neuroscientists, and high-tech educators tend to see us as just a collection of apps, which can be tested through our quick response time, in reality,

136 THE DEATH OF THE LIBERAL CLASSROOM

we are embodied humans with an integrated mind and the possibility of free will, creativity, and deliberate reason.[58]

Another driving force behind the downsizing of expertise and the rise of libertarian economics is the role played by the Web. As a decentralized system catering to user-generated media, the Internet has opened the door for the triumph of the amateur and the degrading of modern institutions like universities, newspapers, bookstores, "value-free" science, and museums. Some of these transformations may be very beneficial, but they do point to a general tendency to transform occupations into hobbies or cheap labor. Moreover, the emerging libertarian consensus makes it hard to imagine how we can ever solve most of our pressing social, political, and economic problems. As the free market mimics natural selection and computer networks replicate our neural connections, our current social inequalities become naturalized and taken for granted.

Notes

1 D'Souza, Dinesh. *Illiberal education: The politics of race and sex on campus.* New York: Free Press, 1991; Horowitz, David. *The professors: The 101 most dangerous academics in America.* Washington: Regnery, 2006.

2 Frank, Thomas. *What's the matter with Kansas?: How conservatives won the heart of America.* Macmillan, 2007.

3 Washburn, Jennifer. *University, Inc.: The corporate corruption of higher education.* Basic Books, 2008.

4 Kurtz, Howard. "College faculties a most liberal lot, study finds." *Washington Post* 3.29 (2005): 05. www.washingtonpost.com/wp-dyn/articles/A8427-2005Mar28.html.

5 Clancy, Patrick, and Gaële Goastellec. "Exploring access and equity in higher education: Policy and performance in a comparative perspective." *Higher Education Quarterly* 61.2 (2007): 136–154.

6 Chemerinsky, Erwin. "Is tenure necessary to protect academic freedom?." *American Behavioral Scientist* 41.5 (1998): 638–651. www.americanbar.org/content/dam/aba/migrated/2011_build/legal_education/committees/standards_review_documents/20110609_comment_security_of_position_erwin_chemerinsky.authcheckdam.pdf.

7 Kezar, Adrianna, Jaime Lester, and Gregory Anderson. "Challenging stereotypes that interfere with effective governance." *Thought & Action* (2006): 121.www.nea.org/assets/img/PubThoughtAndAction/TAA_06_12.pdf.

THE DEATH OF THE LIBERAL CLASSROOM   137

8 Simmons, Daniel. "The death of UC faculty salary scales." http://academicsenate.ucdavis.edu/local_resources/docs/archive/06_death_uc_salaries.pdf.

9 Newfield, Christopher. *Unmaking the public university: The forty-year assault on the middle class.* Harvard University Press, 2008; Wilson, John K. *The myth of political correctness: The conservative attack on higher education.* Duke University Press, 1995.

10 Horowitz, David. *The professors: The 101 most dangerous academics in America.* Regnery Publishing, 2006.

11 Kirp, David L. *Shakespeare, Einstein, and the bottom line: The marketing of higher education.* Harvard University Press, 2009.

12 Hedges, Chris. *Death of the liberal class.* Vintage Books Canada, 2011.

13 Nisbet, Robert A. *The degradation of the academic dogma.* Transaction Publishers, 1971.

14 Giroux, Henry. *Neoliberalism's war on higher education.* Haymarket Books, 2014: 18.

15 Ibid., 19.

16 Giroux, 20.

17 Ibid.

18 Ibid., 27.

19 Ibid., 35.

20 Ibid., 43.

21 Freire, Paulo. *Pedagogy of the oppressed.* Bloomsbury Publishing, 2000.

22 Hedges, Chris. *Death of the liberal class.* Nation Books, 2010.

23 Giroux, 72.

24 Magill Jr, R. Jay. *Chic ironic bitterness.* University of Michigan Press, 2009.

25 Giroux's self-contradictory nature comes out when he declares that "our intellectual allegiances should be less concerned with ideological dogmatism." The problem here is that he often comes off as highly ideological and dogmatic, and so it is as if he protests too much against ideological purity in order to protect himself from being accused of being an ideologue. Ibid., 98.

26 Ibid., 99.

27 Ibid., 118.

28 Satel, Sally, and Scott O. Lilienfeld. *Brainwashed: The seductive appeal of mindless neuroscience.* Basic Books, 2013; Tallis, R. "Aping mankind: Neuromania." *Darwinitis and the misrepresentation of humanity.* Acumen, 2011.

29 Cosmides, Leda, and John Tooby. "Evolutionary psychology: A primer." *Evolutionary psychology: A primer* (1997).

30 Haseltine, Eric. "Changing your brain's factory settings." www.huffingtonpost.com/eric-haseltine/changing-your-brains-fact_b_738949.html.

31 A survey of recent neuroscience can be found in Kaku, Michio. *The future of the mind: The scientific quest to understand, enhance, and empower the mind.* Random House LLC, 2014.

138   THE DEATH OF THE LIBERAL CLASSROOM

32 As Raymond Tallis argues in his book *Aping Mankind*, one of the key moves of neuroscience is to equate our brains with our minds in order to argue that we are essentially computers preprogrammed through evolution. To prove the identity of the mind and the brain, neuroscientists use brain scanning technologies like fMRIs to show how when people look at a certain object or think about a certain emotion, a specific part of their brain is activated. For example, a person will be shown a picture of a rat, and neural activity will be registered by an fMRI in the prefrontal lobes. The conclusion that is drawn from this is that our instinctual disgust of rats is located in a specific region of the brain and connected to a certain chemical neurotransmitter derived from an evolutionary inheritance. However, as Tallis and many others have shown, it takes an fMRI about 2-10 seconds to register a change in blood flow, while the neural reactions take less than a millisecond. Furthermore, an fMRI can only register activity at a high level, and thus a lot of other neural activities and locations are missed by these machines.

In the desire to match a state of consciousness with a brain location and a specific chemical, neuroscientists often fail to register that the brain is an integrated neural circuit with multiple networks that connect and disconnect different parts of the brain. In fact, if we examine recent theories of computer science and cognitive processing, we find that neural networks are: decentralized, distributed, redundant, over-determined, and differential. Unfortunately, if you read many current accounts of neuroscience, this complex model is often discarded in order to stress isolated parts of the brain related to specific chemicals and inherited traits.

Some have called this reductive tendency neuromania or Darwinitis, and there is much evidence that these scientific moves are motivated by how research is funded inside and outside of research universities. Not only is it easier to get a big grant to study a part of the human mind if you tie it to a particular technology and brain location, but drug companies often in conjunction with the federal government also favor research that points to a specific neurotransmitter because the pathway to pharmaceutical intervention is clearer. Moreover, university researchers have reported that once a program purchases expensive equipment, like an fMRI, researchers are pushed to use this specific technology as it dries up all other sources of funding.

33 The hostility of evolutionary psychologists to the social sciences can be seen in the following passage from "Evolutionary Psychology: A Primer.": Both before and after Darwin, a common view among philosophers and scientists has been that the human mind resembles a blank slate, virtually free of content until written on by the hand of experience. According to Aquinas, there is "nothing in the intellect which was not previously in the senses." Working within this framework, the British Empiricists and their successors produced elaborate theories about how

THE DEATH OF THE LIBERAL CLASSROOM 139

experience, refracted through a small handful of innate mental procedures, inscribed content onto the mental slate. David Hume's view was typical, and set the pattern for many later psychological and social science theories: "...there appear to be only three principles of connexion among ideas, namely *Resemblance, Contiguity* in time or place, and *Cause* or *Effect*."

Over the years, the technological metaphor used to describe the structure of the human mind has been consistently updated, from blank slate to switchboard to general purpose computer, but the central tenet of these Empiricist views has remained the same. Indeed, it has become the reigning orthodoxy in mainstream anthropology, sociology, and most areas of psychology. According to this orthodoxy, all of the specific content of the human mind originally derives from the "outside"—from the environment and the social world—and the evolved architecture of the mind consists solely or predominantly of a small number of general purpose mechanisms that are content-independent, and which sail under names such as "learning," "induction," "intelligence," "imitation," "rationality," "the capacity for culture," or simply "culture."

According to this view, the same mechanisms are thought to govern how one acquires a language, how one learns to recognize emotional expressions, how one thinks about incest, or how one acquires ideas and attitudes about friends and reciprocity—everything but perception. This is because the mechanisms that govern reasoning, learning, and memory are assumed to operate uniformly, according to unchanging principles, regardless of the content they are operating on or the larger category or domain involved. (For this reason, they are described as *content-independent* or *domain-general*.) Such mechanisms, by definition, have no pre-existing content built-in to their procedures, they are not designed to construct certain contents more readily than others, and they have no features specialized for processing particular kinds of content. Since these hypothetical mental mechanisms have no content to impart, it follows that all the particulars of what we think and feel derive externally, from the physical and social world. The social world organizes and injects meaning into individual minds, but our universal human psychological architecture has no distinctive structure that organizes the social world or imbues it with characteristic meanings. According to this familiar view—what we have elsewhere called the Standard Social Science Model—the contents of human minds are primarily (or entirely) free social constructions, and the social sciences are autonomous and disconnected from any evolutionary or psychological foundation (Tooby & Cosmides, 1992).[59]

Three decades of progress and convergence in cognitive psychology, evolutionary biology, and neuroscience have shown that this view of the human mind is radically defective. Evolutionary psychology provides an alternative framework that is beginning to replace it. On this view, all normal human minds reliably develop a standard collection of reasoning and regulatory circuits that are functionally specialized and, frequently, domain-specific. These circuits organize the way we interpret our experiences, inject certain recurrent concepts and motivations into our mental life, and provide universal frames of meaning that allow us to understand the actions and intentions of others. Beneath the level of surface variability, all humans share certain views and assumptions about the nature of the world and human action by virtue of these human universal reasoning circuits.

34 Petersen, Michael Bang, et al. "Who deserves help? Evolutionary psychology, social emotions, and public opinion about welfare." *Political Psychology* 33.3 (2012): 395–418.

35 Ibid.

36 Logue, A. W. "Evolutionary theory and the psychology of eating." *Baruch College, City University of New York* (1998). http://faculty.baruch.cuny.edu/naturalscience/biology/darwin/faculty/LogueA.html#uncertain.

37 Braconnier, Deborah. "Social hierarchy prewired in the brain." http://medicalxpress.com/news/2011-09-social-hierarchy-prewired-brain.html.

38 Pinker, Steven. *The blank slate: The modern denial of human nature.* Penguin, 2003.

39 Ibid., 435–439.

40 von Hayek, Friedrich August. "The pretence of knowledge." *The American Economic Review* (1989): 3–7.

41 James, Surowiecki. "The wisdom of the crowds." (2004).

42 In a previous book, I argue that the real new political consensus is the role of libertarianism on the Right and the Left. Samuels, Robert. "New media, cultural studies, and critical theory after postmodernism: Automodernity from Žižek to Laclau." (2010).

43 Reiss, Steven, and James Wiltz. "Why people watch reality TV." *Media Psychology* 6.4 (2004): 363–378.

44 Davidson, Cathy N. *Now you see it: How the brain science of attention will transform the way we live, work, and learn.* New York, NY: Viking, 2011: 88.

45 Ibid., 2.

46 Terranova, Tiziana. "Free labor: Producing culture for the digital economy." *Social Text* 18.2 (2000): 33–58.

47 Davidson cites Hayek as an important theorist of the new Web economy, 229.

48 Ibid., 45.

49 Bruce Kaufman in Ross B. Emmett, ed. *The elgar companion to the Chicago school of economics* (2010): 133.

50 NewsHour, P. B. S. "Greenspan admits 'flaw' to Congress, predicts more economic problems." (2011). www.pbs.org/newshour/bb/business-july-dec08-crisishearing_10-23/.

51 Davidson, 162.

THE DEATH OF THE LIBERAL CLASSROOM 141

52 Durand, Rodolphe, and Vicente Vargas. "Ownership, organization, and private firms' efficient use of resources." *Strategic Management Journal* 24.7 (2003): 667–675.

53 Davidson, 65.

54 Ibid., 110.

55 Ibid., 209.

56 Watters, Audrey. "The problems with peer grading in coursera." *Inside Higher Education* (2012). www.insidehighered.com/blogs/hack-higher-education/problems-peer-grading-coursera#sthash.dH0WhEwA.dpbs.

57 Soares, Louis. "A 'disruptive' look at competency-based education: How the innovative use of technology will transform the college experience." *Center for American Progress. June* (2012).http://americanprogress.org/issues/higher-education/report/2012/06/07/11680/a-disruptive-look-at-competency-based-education/.

58 For a critique of the loss of free will in neuroscience, see McGilchrist, Iain. *The master and his emissary: The divided brain and the making of the western world.* Yale University Press, 2009.

59 Cosmides, Leda, and John Tooby. "Cognitive adaptations for social exchange." *The Adapted Mind* (1992): 163–228.

8

WILL TECHNOLOGY AND THE FREE MARKET SAVE HIGHER ED AND THE JOB MARKET?

In the last few chapters, we have seen that a shared set of myths on the Left and the Right has positioned higher education to be the solution to most of our economic and social problems. Beliefs in meritocracy, the invisible hand, and social Darwinism all tend to support the notion that an unregulated free market system is the best way to allow free individuals to contribute to the common good. However, the investment in this libertarian ideology often blinds people from seeing how meritocracies can quickly turn back into aristocracies, and the pursuit of rational self-interest can destroy the common good. Moreover, as universities present themselves as the engines of social mobility and economic advancement, they often are shaped by the power and privilege of the wealthy. According to the logic of neoliberalism, the solution to these social inequalities is to reinvest in the free market and to privatize all public institutions so that government planning and regulation do not get in the way of innovation and economic competition.[1]

In the realm of higher education, neoliberalism is related to the development of for-profit colleges and online education: the idea here is that if schools have to compete for students in an open market, they can become more efficient and affordable, especially if they turn to technology to teach a large number of students at the same time.[2] The proponents of this neoliberal strategy argue that traditional public institutions are too slow to innovate, and they are dominated by unneeded regulations and price controls, and so the dynamism and rationality of the free market are blocked. Yet, if we look at the reality of the situation, we find that online for-profit institutions like the University of Phoenix have not lowered the costs for the students, and they have had to rely on public student loans and grants in order to stay in business.[3] Furthermore, many of these for-profit colleges have spent a great deal of their money catering to low-income, minority students who most often end up without a degree or a job but are prone to high levels of debt.[4] It is also important to stress that some of these schools turn a huge profit for their managers and investors, but virtually all of the faculty are part-time without job security and receive very low wages.[5] These schools therefore represent a microcosm of the post-Great Recession economy where profits are horded at the top, while most of the workers have been de-professionalized and suffer from underemployment. Meanwhile, as public institutions are marketized, public funds support private profit.

Post-recession Massive Open Online Courses

At the same moment that we have seen a tremendous growth in for-profit colleges, we have also witnessed efforts by state governments to promote online education as a way of making higher education more affordable and accessible. For example, in California, after years of state budget cuts to the higher education systems, several high-ranking public officials tried to push through a bill that would have forced universities and colleges to share a common set of online courses developed in part by for-profit providers.[6] The logic behind this bipartisan push for technology-based education begins with the idea that the public support for higher education will never return to its past high levels, so schools have to learn how to do more with less, and online education is the magic solution to this problem.

Like many other neoliberal strategies, the starting point is often scarcity and a sense of crisis. In other words, because we do not think that we will ever return to our old way of supporting these public institutions, they will always be underfunded, and this lack of support will generate a continuous crisis, and

144   SAVING THE JOB MARKET?

in response to the crisis, new things have to be tried.[7] The next step is to say that technology is always new and innovative, and so the solutions have to come from the ability of new media to make everything more accessible and less expensive. This logic can be found in a report made by the Little Hoover Commission in California:

> all three segments of our higher education system—community colleges, the California State University and the University of California—have so far failed to lead in the promising area of online education. There have been some recent improvements, particularly in the CSU system, but other universities, including Stanford, Harvard and MIT, have more aggressively experimented with online options. It seems as though our state, once the innovator, has become a reluctant follower. While online won't by itself be a panacea, it almost certainly must be part of the mix as our state and nation struggle to prepare more and more young people for the jobs of the future.[8]

One of the assumptions underlying this argument is that universities must follow what other institutions and innovators are doing, and if they fail to "aggressively experiment," they will be left in the dust. There is a combination here of social Darwinism and cynical conformity: universities and colleges must do what others are doing, not because it is necessarily the right thing to do, but because they do not want to be beaten out in the competition by the institutions that are the fastest to adopt to the new environment.

Later on in the same report by the Little Hoover Commission, the tone turns more urgent:

> Online education is emerging as an important technology, and one that holds great promise of increasing access to higher education and the potential to lower costs. Failure to adapt could put existing state institutions at a competitive and cost disadvantage. The Commission recognizes that there have been limited online offerings in the past,

SAVING THE JOB MARKET?

but not at the scale that will be necessary to address the burgeoning needs of the expanding technologically-savvy student body. It appears as though California is moving substantially slower than it should to integrate online because of faculty opposition and/or general inertia.[9]

Once again, education is turned into a race between competing institutions that are all trying to out-innovate each other. This social Darwinian logic is coupled with the myth that since current students have grown up using computers, they naturally would want to have their education online. However, several polls and studies have actually shown the opposite: although students are constantly using new technologies in their social lives, they prefer to have in-person classes.[10]

The push for online education has also resulted in a constant blurring of the lines between public and private entities. For instance, in one of its main recommendations for the state government, the Little Hoover Commission report calls for more public funding of mixed private-public online ventures:

> The Legislature should provide incentives for developing online courses for high-demand introductory courses, bottleneck prerequisite courses and remedial courses that demonstrate effective learning. To qualify, the course must be able to be awarded course and unit credit, at a minimum, at all California community colleges, or all California state universities, or all campuses of the University of California. Better yet would be courses that would be awarded credit at any campuses of all three segments. Courses could be designed by private or non-profit entities according to college and university criteria.[11]

By using taxpayer dollars at public institutions to hire outside private and nonprofit companies to design courses, the commission feeds into the neoliberal strategy of transferring public funds to private concerns. Here, the profits will be privatized, but the potential risks are socialized. In other words, the private providers

146 SAVING THE JOB MARKET?

will make money no matter what, but if the online courses end up costing more than they bring in, the public institutions have to cover the losses.[12]

Another related aspect of the neoliberal higher education agenda is to stress the efficiency of the systems over the quality of the education. We find this logic at play in the commission's discussion of the need to increase graduation rates:

> From the state's perspective, the only way to meet the projected need for graduates is to increase the number of Californians who finish a given course of higher education study, with either a certificate, associate's degree or four-year degree and reduce time to graduation so that a graduate can more quickly free up space for students on the way up—without vastly scaling up the existing higher education infrastructure. It may mean making more sections of high demand classes available, in person or online, so that students blocked out of classes they want do not have to take classes they don't want simply to remain eligible for scholarships, grants and loans. The state simply does not have the money to reach projected needs by looking at education spending on a cost-per-student basis.[13]

Embedded in this argument is the idea that California needs to increase its number of college graduates in order to fill all of the new high-tech jobs, and so the key is to use technology to move people through the system in a faster and less costly manner. One of the problems with this logic is that online courses often have a much higher dropout rate than traditional courses, and the production and circulation of these high-tech courses can be quite costly.[14] Moreover, what this report does not mention is that the main reason students are having a hard time getting the classes that they need to graduate on time is that universities and colleges are short-changing undergraduate instruction.[15] As we have seen, public universities and colleges have seen their funding reduced by state budget cuts, and at the same time, these schools have poured their money into other activities, like administration and the amenities arms race. In fact, universities have driven down the

SAVING THE JOB MARKET? 147

cost of instruction by using large lecture classes and inexpensive part-time faculty, and so it is unlikely that the turn to online education will save any money, and it is more likely that it will actually increase the cost of administration, staffing, and infrastructure.

As the commission report itself points out, one thing that is for sure is that the turn to online education and outside for-profit providers will transform institutions of higher education:

> The rise of the Massive Open Online Courses (MOOCs) brings with it the promise of increased access and potentially lower cost. MOOCs also hold the potential to unbundle previously packaged courses of study, much as cell phones and voice-over-Internet protocol unbundled telephone service, and Craigslist and online news aggregators dismantled the newspaper industry, and online file sharing undermined the recording industry and music retailing. Though previous rationales for reconstructing the Master Plan remain as urgent as ever, the disruptive potential of MOOCs, if not addressed constructively through a coordinated and efficient strategy, suggests that delaying an overhaul of the Master Plan creates an immense risk not only to California's public higher education institutions, but to the state's long-term economic and civic vitality.[16]

Like so many neoliberal pushes for privatization through technological disruption, this report uses the threat of an "immense risk" to push politicians and school officials to embrace innovation and the "debundling" of the academic profession. In other words, instead of seeing the faculty as teachers, researchers, and administrators, all of these tasks need to be separated so that the managers can make the decisions and the low-paid teachers, who are no longer involved in the research mission, can become course facilitators. Of course, this debundling also helps to push de-professionalization and an increased gap between the pay of the managers and the income of the workers. In fact, one can read the passage above as saying that just as many good jobs in the areas of music, journalism, and communication have been

148   SAVING THE JOB MARKET?

downsized, universities and colleges should pursue the same self-destructive logic.

The Darwinian Innovation Myth

Underlying the neoliberal push for innovation in higher education is often a logic of social Darwinism, which states that institutions must enter a free market competition where only the strongest survive. As Jill Lepore writes in her article, "The Disruption Machine," our current economy is dominated by the logic of technological and economic disruption:

> The eighteenth century embraced the idea of progress; the nineteenth century had evolution; the twentieth century had growth and then innovation. Our era has disruption, which, despite its futurism, is atavistic. It's a theory of history founded on a profound anxiety about financial collapse, an apocalyptic fear of global devastation, and shaky evidence.[17]

In the logic of the shock doctrine and crisis capitalism, the new myth of Darwinian disruption is founded on the idea that only a radical break with current practices can allow us to handle the economics of scarcity. In fact, one can understand much of the political appeal of Donald Trump as the embodiment of disruptive capitalism and the downsizing of expertise. Not only did people vote for him because he would shake things up, but they also felt that he was an outsider and not an establishment elite with snobby expertise.

For Lepore, underlying this push for disruption is a desire to escape criticism and responsibility as a neoliberal agenda is imposed:

> Most big ideas have loud critics. Not disruption. Disruptive innovation as the explanation for how change happens has been subject to little serious criticism, partly because it's headlong, while critical inquiry is unhurried; partly because disrupters ridicule doubters by charging them with fogyism, as if to criticize a theory of change were identical to decrying change;

SAVING THE JOB MARKET?

149

and partly because, in its modern usage, innovation is the idea of progress jammed into a criticism-proof jack-in-the-box.[18]

We see this rejection of criticism in favor of fast-paced innovation when politicians and higher ed entrepreneurs blame faculty and shared governance for slowing down the adoption of new technological fixes. For example, the Little Hoover Commission states the following: "It appears as though California is moving substantially slower than it should to integrate online because of faculty opposition and/or general inertia."[19] A common theme in the rhetoric of online education and the myth of disruption is that professors do not want to embrace these new technological fixes because they are afraid of losing their power and jobs. Of course, faculty should be concerned because underlying this discourse is the idea that costs can be reduced by debundling the professor and replacing current workers with free labor, international outsourcing, and part-time workers.

Lepore argues that the new myth of disruption also helps to overcome some of the problems with technological progress that became apparent in the twentieth century:

> The idea of progress—the notion that human history is the history of human betterment—dominated the world view of the West between the Enlightenment and the First World War. It had critics from the start, and, in the last century, even people who cherish the idea of progress, and point to improvements like the eradication of contagious diseases and the education of girls, have been hard-pressed to hold on to it while reckoning with two World Wars, the Holocaust and Hiroshima, genocide and global warming. Replacing "progress" with "innovation" skirts the question of whether a novelty is an improvement: the world may not be getting better and better but our devices are getting newer and newer.[20]

This stress on innovation over progress can be found throughout higher education where one rarely addresses the question

150   SAVING THE JOB MARKET?

of the quality of learning and teaching, and instead, the driving force appears to be change for change sake.

Lepore argues that this push for innovation and disruption is coming largely from elite university business schools:

> Disruptive innovation as an explanation for how change happens is everywhere. Ideas that come from business schools are exceptionally well marketed. Faith in disruption is the best illustration, and the worst case, of a larger historical transformation having to do with secularization, and what happens when the invisible hand replaces the hand of God as explanation and justification.[21]

Here, we see how supposedly liberal institutions are leading the neoliberal libertarian invisible hand myth: one of the moves here is to replace the self-interested individual with the self-interested institution as the driving force behind the magical translation of selfishness into the common good.

Perhaps the key move of neoliberalism is the idea that market logic can be applied to all aspects of human existence:

> Innovation and disruption are ideas that originated in the arena of business but which have since been applied to arenas whose values and goals are remote from the values and goals of business. People aren't disk drives. Public schools, colleges and universities, churches, museums, and many hospitals, all of which have been subjected to disruptive innovation, have revenues and expenses and infrastructures, but they aren't industries in the same way that manufacturers of hard-disk drives or truck engines or drygoods are industries. Journalism isn't an industry in that sense, either.[22]

In terms of jobs and economic inequality, what we have witnessed since the 1970s is in part the result of this idea that all public and democratic institutions work best when they are subjected to market discipline and the creative destruction of Darwinian economics. Yet, as Lepore stresses, there is a great difference between private and public concerns:

Doctors have obligations to their patients, teachers to their students, pastors to their congregations, curators to the public, and journalists to their readers—obligations that lie outside the realm of earnings, and are fundamentally different from the obligations that a business executive has to employees, partners, and investors. Historically, institutions like museums, hospitals, schools, and universities have been supported by patronage, donations made by individuals or funding from church or state.[23]

Thus, as the public funding for public institutions has been reduced, the logic of neoliberal economics has taken hold, and older models of obligation and concern have been eliminated.

The Darwinian University

In turning to how the logic of disruption applies to higher education, Lepore focuses on the work of Christensen and Eyring's "The Innovative University," which serves as a good reference point for the myth that the free market and new technologies will make higher education more affordable and accessible:

On the basis of this research, Christensen and Eyring's recommendations for the disruption of the modern university include a "mix of face-to-face and online learning." The publication of "The Innovative University," in 2011, contributed to a frenzy for Massive Open Online Courses, or MOOCs, at colleges and universities across the country, including a collaboration between Harvard and M.I.T., which was announced in May of 2012. Shortly afterward, the University of Virginia's panicked board of trustees attempted to fire the president, charging her with jeopardizing the institution's future by failing to disruptively innovate with sufficient speed; the vice-chair of the board forwarded to the chair a *Times* column written by David Brooks, "The Campus Tsunami," in which he cited Christensen.[24]

As Lepore documents, the logic and myths of neoliberal disruption were first generated in university business schools, and then

152   SAVING THE JOB MARKET?

they moved to for-profit companies and next to the mainstream media. The result is an echo chamber of ideological repetition that serves to naturalize the constructed rhetoric of innovate or die.

In looking at Christensen and Eyring's "The Innovative University," we see how university professors themselves have helped to circulate an antiuniversity discourse: "In the absence of a disruptive new technology, the combination of prestige and loyal support from donors and legislators has allowed traditional universities to weather occasional storms. Fundamental change has been unnecessary."[25] According to this neoliberal argument, universities have gotten away with doing things the same way for such a long time because they have received generous support from the government and private donors, but times are changing, and these schools can no longer hide their inefficiencies behind a cloak of excessive funding:

> That is no longer true, though, for any but a relative handful of institutions. Costs have risen to unprecedented heights, and new competitors are emerging. A disruptive technology, online learning, is at work in higher education, allowing both for-profit and traditional not-for-profit institutions to rethink the entire traditional higher education model. Private universities without national recognition and large endowments are at great financial risk. So are public universities, even prestigious ones such as the University of California at Berkeley.[26]

One of the ideas here is that public universities will never regain their past public support so they will be forced to innovate in order to stay in business, but wealthy private universities, like Christensen's Harvard, have enough money to resist change.

From the bottom-line perspective of neoliberal social Darwinism, the free market will force public universities and non-wealthy private schools to turn to cheap online education to stay competitive:

> For the vast majority of universities change is inevitable. The main questions are when it will occur and what forces will bring it about. It would be unfortunate if internal delay

caused change to come through external regulation or pressure from newer, nimbler competitors. Until now, American higher education has largely regulated itself, to great effect. U.S. universities are among the most lightly regulated by government. They are free to choose what discoveries to pursue and what subjects to teach, without concern for economic or political agendas. Responsibly exercised, this freedom is a great intellectual and competitive advantage.[27]

On the one hand, these authors argue that the lack of governmental regulation and the high level of institutional freedom have helped American universities become the best in the world; however, on the other hand, the twin myths of austerity and Darwinian competition undermine the traditional freedom of these institutions.

Like many other advocates of neoliberal innovation, Christensen uses the biological theory of evolution to naturalize the formation of social institutions:

University DNA is not only similar across institutions, it is also highly stable, having evolved over hundreds of years. Replication of the DNA occurs continuously, as each retiring employee or graduating student is replaced by someone screened against the same criteria applied to his or her predecessor. The way things are done is determined not by individual preference but by institutional procedure written into the genetic code. Yet the university's steadiness is also why one cannot make it more responsive to modern economic and social realities merely by regulating its behavior. The genetic tendencies are too strong. The institutional genes expressed in course catalogs and in standards for admitting students and promoting faculty are selfish, replicating themselves faithfully even at the expense of the institution's welfare. A university cannot be made more efficient by simply cutting its operating budget, any more than a carnivore can be converted to an herbivore by constraining its intake of meat. Nor can universities be made by legislative fiat to perform functions for which they are not expressly designed. For example, requiring

154　　SAVING THE JOB MARKET?

universities to admit underprepared students is unlikely to produce a proportional number of new college graduates. It is not in the typical university's genetic makeup to remediate such students, and neither regulation nor economic pressure will be enough, alone, to change that.[28]

As I argued in the last chapter, this confusing of social structures and biological processes serves a dual process: on the one hand, it makes the social institutions appear to be natural and inevitable, and, on the other hand, it shows natural processes to be technological and thus open to change and disruption.

The MOOC Myth

The theories and myths behind high-tech, higher ed innovation and disruption that I have been discussing can be fleshed out by seeing how one of the main promoters of MOOCs has tried to sell the public on the need to adopt this new technological mode of higher education. In her TED Talk, Daphne Koller, one of the founders of Coursera, begins by connecting with the audience over their shared privilege of going to college during a time when it was not being disrupted or defunded:

> Like many of you, I'm one of the lucky people. I was born to a family where education was pervasive. I'm a third-generation PhD, a daughter of two academics. In my childhood, I played around in my father's university lab. So it was taken for granted that I attend some of the best universities, which in turn opened the door to a world of opportunity.[29]

Here, we refind the familiar story of a university-based faculty member pointing out how much she benefited from the traditional elite university, but we are soon told that this old meritocratic system is no longer tenable, and thus the ladder that she climbed up on has to be pulled away and replaced with a new technology of social mobility:

> Unfortunately, most of the people in the world are not so lucky. In some parts of the world, for example, South Africa,

SAVING THE JOB MARKET?

education is just not readily accessible. In South Africa, the educational system was constructed in the days of apartheid for the white minority. And as a consequence, today there are just not enough spots for the many more people who want and deserve a high-quality education. That scarcity led to a crisis in January of this year at the University of Johannesburg. There were a handful of positions left open from the standard admissions process, and the night before they were supposed to open that for registration, thousands of people lined up outside the gate in a line a mile long, hoping to be first in line to get one of those positions. When the gates opened, there was a stampede, and 20 people were injured and one woman died. She was a mother who gave her life trying to get her son a chance at a better life.[30]

By turning to a tragic story of scarcity, Koller is able to position her new private provider of educational goods as a progressive company dedicated to making higher education more affordable and accessible.

In a repetition of the key myths that have been discussed throughout this book, Koller argues both that higher education is not affordable because of the cost of delivering the courses and that we need to make it more affordable so that more people can compete for jobs requiring a college degree:

But even in parts of the world like the United States where education is available, it might not be within reach. There has been much discussed in the last few years about the rising cost of health care. What might not be quite as obvious to people is that during that same period the cost of higher education tuition has been increasing at almost twice the rate, for a total of 559 percent since 1985. This makes education unaffordable for many people. Finally, even for those who do manage to get the higher education, the doors of opportunity might not open. Only a little over half of recent college graduates in the United States who get a higher education actually are working in jobs that require that education. This, of course, is not true for the students who graduate from the top institutions, but for many others, they do not get the value for their time and their effort.[31]

The major contradiction in this analysis is the idea that we need to produce more people with higher ed degrees, but half of the current people with degrees are already working at jobs that do not require college degrees. This contradiction stems from the myth that college attainment is the solution to all of our economic and social problems.

One of the myths guiding the new push for online education is the idea that companies like Coursera improve the quality of higher education by putting the best teachers in front of the highest number of students:

> we needed to really try and scale this up, to bring the best quality education to as many people as we could. So we formed Coursera, whose goal is to take the best courses from the best instructors at the best universities and provide it to everyone around the world for free.[32]

The first issue here is the idea that Coursera knows who the best professors are and that they can use these teachers by simply putting their lectures online. As professors from San Jose State University argued, one of the problems with this model is that it creates a situation where students at nonelite schools have to passively listen to academic stars without any possibility of interacting with their own education.[33] A related issue is the idea that these courses are free to produce, when, in reality, these professors are using funding and support from their elite institutions to prepare, produce, and circulate their lectures.

Although most MOOC courses do not allow the students to receive course credit at their home institutions, the promoters of this new online fad argue for a new form of higher ed credentialing:

> At the end of the course, the students got a certificate. They could present that certificate to a prospective employer and get a better job, and we know many students who did. Some students took their certificate and presented this to an

SAVING THE JOB MARKET?

educational institution at which they were enrolled for actual college credit. So these students were really getting something meaningful for their investment of time and effort.[34]

One problem with this new model for college certification is that many employers don't respect the value of this online form of education, and they still want to hire people with real degrees.[35] Another strategy that promoters of MOOCs like to present is the idea that the current model of higher education is so bad that it can only be improved by putting the courses online:

> This is a kind of simple question that I as an instructor might ask in class, but when I ask that kind of a question in class, 80 percent of the students are still scribbling the last thing I said, 15 percent are zoned out on Facebook, and then there's the smarty pants in the front row who blurts out the answer before anyone else has had a chance to think about it, and I as the instructor am terribly gratified that somebody actually knew the answer. And so the lecture moves on before, really, most of the students have even noticed that a question had been asked. Here, every single student has to engage with the material.[36]

Like so many other MOOC enthusiasts, Koller shows the value of online education by comparing it to the worst type of traditional higher education. Thus, instead of calling for smaller, interactive classes that really challenge each individual student, the strategy here is to mock the current state of education and provide a low-cost alternative.

Of course, the main way that MOOCs attempt to reduce costs is to reduce the need for faculty and graduate teaching assistants:

> And of course these simple retrieval questions are not the end of the story. One needs to build in much more meaningful practice questions, and one also needs to provide the students with feedback on those questions. Now, how do you grade the work of 100,000 students if you do not have 10,000 TAs? The answer is, you need to use technology to do it for you. Now, fortunately, technology has come a long way, and we can now

158   SAVING THE JOB MARKET?

grade a range of interesting types of homework. In addition to multiple choice and the kinds of short answer questions that you saw in the video, we can also grade math, mathematical expressions as well as mathematical derivations. We can grade models, whether it's financial models in a business class or physical models in a science or engineering class and we can grade some pretty sophisticated programming assignments.[37]

In other words, like so many new high-tech companies, the idea is to replace current workers with machines. Although this may reduce some of the costs, the result is that job opportunities are also reduced as the quality of education goes down.

At one point in her lecture, Koller admits that this type of teaching and grading does not allow for the critical thinking that is often valued in the humanities and social sciences, and so the solution is to turn the students into free laborers:

So we had to come up with a different solution. And the solution we ended up using is peer grading. It turns out that previous studies show, like this one by Saddler and Good, that peer grading is a surprisingly effective strategy for providing reproducible grades. It was tried only in small classes, but there it showed, for example, that these student-assigned grades on the y-axis are actually very well correlated with the teacher-assigned grade on the x-axis. What's even more surprising is that self-grades, where the students grade their own work critically—so long as you incentivize them properly so they can't give themselves a perfect score—are actually even better correlated with the teacher grades. And so this is an effective strategy that can be used for grading at scale, and is also a useful learning strategy for the students, because they actually learn from the experience. So we now have the largest peer-grading pipeline ever devised, where tens of thousands of students are grading each other's work, and quite successfully, I have to say.[38]

SAVING THE JOB MARKET? 159

This notion of peer grading has been severely criticized, but what is often not analyzed is the idea that these university professors are trying to put most teachers and graduate student instructors out of business. In other words, higher education is used here as a method to increase unemployment and underemployment.

To help eliminate the professor as educational middleman, one idea is to just have the students teach each other:

> Students collaborated in these courses in a variety of different ways. First of all, there was a question and answer forum, where students would pose questions, and other students would answer those questions. And the really amazing thing is, because there were so many students, it means that even if a student posed a question at 3 o'clock in the morning, somewhere around the world, there would be somebody who was awake and working on the same problem. And so, in many of our courses, the median response time for a question on the question and answer forum was 22 minutes. Which is not a level of service I have ever offered to my Stanford students.[39]

Once again, the celebration of the online course is coupled with a mockery of this professor's own institution. Instead of students getting high-quality, in-person education from expert faculty, they are being told that they should just rely on each other to read and grade their work.

In the logic of the invisible hand and the bottom-up, self-regulating rhetoric of libertarian economics, we are told that students can teach and organize themselves in a spontaneous fashion:

> And you can see from the student testimonials that students actually find that because of this large online community, they got to interact with each other in many ways that were deeper than they did in the context of the physical classroom. Students also self-assembled, without any kind of intervention from us, into small study groups.[40]

160 SAVING THE JOB MARKET?

Like the magic of the free market, the ideology here revolves around the notion that experts, planners, and professionals are no longer needed in a new media economy that celebrates the amateur at the expense of the paid professional. Higher education is positioned to be a leader in the creative destruction of professional employment.

Not only are students told that they should just teach and grade themselves, but they should also become data that can be later packaged and sold on the open market. In fact, just as Facebook and Amazon motivate people to voluntarily give up their private information so that it can be sold to marketers, corporate promoters of MOOCs hide their strategy for monetization behind the veil of providing a social good:

> There are some tremendous opportunities to be had from this kind of framework. The first is that it has the potential of giving us a completely unprecedented look into understanding human learning. Because the data that we can collect here is unique. You can collect every click, every homework submission, every forum post from tens of thousands of students. So you can turn the study of human learning from the hypothesis-driven mode to the data-driven mode, a transformation that, for example, has revolutionized biology. You can use these data to understand fundamental questions like, what are good learning strategies that are effective versus ones that are not? And in the context of particular courses, you can ask questions like, what are some of the misconceptions that are more common and how do we help students fix them?

Although it appears that the driving force behind this collection of student data is to make learning more effective, it is clear that this use of big data is also a source for future money-making activities.[41] Therefore, like so many other new media companies, at the same time that older professional jobs are being eliminated, capital is accumulated by getting people to freely contribute their labor.

One of the most interesting tricks that MOOC providers perform is the transformation of mass education into highly

SAVING THE JOB MARKET?

personalized learning. The paradox here is that at the same time that people are accessing a class with thousands of other students, they are being told that their education has become more student centered: "So this personalization is something that one can then build by having the virtue of large numbers. Personalization is perhaps one of the biggest opportunities here as well, because it provides us with the potential of solving a 30-year-old problem."[42] Since everyone is sitting alone in front of their computers, mass-produced education appears to be more personal and individualistic, and yet this is done by removing the other person, the teacher, from the equation.

The combination of mass education and highly personalized learning is reliant on the invisible hand and the elimination of social interaction from the learning experience; the idea here is to overcome the modern conflict between society and the individual by using technology as the great mediator:

> Because we cannot afford, as a society, to provide every student with an individual human tutor. But maybe we can afford to provide each student with a computer or a smartphone. So the question is, how can we use technology to push from the left side of the graph, from the blue curve, to the right side with the green curve? Mastery is easy to achieve using a computer, because a computer doesn't get tired of showing you the same video five times. And it doesn't even get tired of grading the same work multiple times, we've seen that in many of the examples that I've shown you. And even personalization is something that we're starting to see the beginnings of, whether it's via the personalized trajectory through the curriculum or some of the personalized feedback that we've shown you.[43]

In this high-tech free market educational system, the public aspect of education is repressed below the smooth interface between the user and the computer, and unlike a real human being, the computer never gets tired, and you do not have to pay it anything.

162 SAVING THE JOB MARKET?

The underlying discourse in this new media evangelism is a debasement and mockery of traditional models of education by people working at traditional institutions of higher education:

> So, if this is so great, are universities now obsolete? Well, Mark Twain certainly thought so. He said that, 'College is a place where a professor's lecture notes go straight to the students' lecture notes, without passing through the brains of either.'

Of course, only elite professors at elite universities have the time and resources to promote a mode of education that reserves in-person learning for the wealthy people who can afford it: everyone else is told that they will have to get their education on the cheap by interacting with computers from the solitude of their own bedrooms.

The Free Market Solution

As the advocates of MOOCs promote the downsizing of the academic labor force and a model of education that increases the inequality between elite universities and everyone else, other higher ed reformers are pushing for a more free market approach. For instance, Richard Vedder from the Center for College Affordability has proposed simply getting rid of financial aid and other governmental interventions in higher education:

> Suppose that the federal government had never enacted the Higher Education Act, and that they had not entered into the business of providing financial assistance to college students. In other words, suppose we had no federal guaranteed student loans, no Pell Grants, no federal work study programs, no higher education tax credits or any other program designed to ostensibly aid students pay for college.[44]

This radical free market solution is based in part on the idea that government support for higher education has allowed colleges and universities to constantly increase tuition. In order, then, to drive down costs, the government should take away all forms of financial aid and loans that help students tolerate increased

SAVING THE JOB MARKET? 163

costs. This solution is based on the assumption that if parents and students refuse to pay inflated prices, the market will force schools to lower their prices and concentrate their spending on essentials. Underlying this argument is the myth that markets always make prices rational by matching supply with demand.

Vedder believes that the removal of financial aid would actually increase the number of low-income students:

> I would predict the proportion of recent college graduates from the bottom quartile of the income distribution would be greater than it actually is today. In other words, the substantial variation of college participation by income would be at least modestly less than today, and higher education would have a somewhat less elitist character to it.[45]

One reason why he thinks that the elimination of aid would help low-income people is that the cost of education would be forced down by market forces: "Lower income persons are more price sensitive than more affluent ones, and high sticker prices have led more lower income persons than higher income ones to say no to college, or pick less expensive options like community colleges."[46] According to the logic of the invisible hand and social Darwinism, people without money will force down the prices of schools no longer receiving financial aid because these low-income students will simply vote with their feet and stop attending these institutions until they lower their prices. Yet, we know that low-income people with aid are already being priced out of many institutions of higher education, and so it does not seem that these schools care if poor students go elsewhere.

This market approach for Vedder would also force schools to reduce the increase in administration and other noninstructional costs:

> we would have a much smaller army of collegiate bureaucrats, what Johns Hopkins' Benjamin Ginsburg calls "deanlets," probably very modestly lower salaries for faculty, possibly greater emphasis on teaching, and fewer, maybe no, million dollar university presidents. Universities and colleges would have smaller

164 SAVING THE JOB MARKET?

budgets, and the total resources devoted to higher education would be tens or scores of billions of dollars less than we in fact spend today. The actual productivity decline in higher education would have not occurred. There would be no talk of a higher education bubble, no U.S. presidents making speeches denouncing university fiscal behavior, or the like.[47]

The idea here is based on the conservative myth that if you reduce the access of funding to an institution, then it will put money into the right places. However, many private businesses that compete in a market system are not always efficient, as we have seen by the high compensation packages of top managers. Moreover, many private colleges and universities that receive very little aid spend a great deal of money on noninstructional activities.

Vedder not only thinks that financial aid allows universities and colleges to raise their tuition, but he also believes that aid undermines student performance:

The connection between university student performance and federal student financial aid is arguably more indirect and subtle, but in my judgment is nonetheless real. The amount of time students spend on academics has declined in tandem with increases in federal student aid programs. Grades have risen with increased student aid—and reduced student academic effort. The Civics Literacy Test of the Intercollegiate Studies Institute and the decennial Adult Literacy Survey of the U.S. Department of Education show that core knowledge and literacy amongst college students are falling. Arum and Roksa compellingly argue that critical thinking and writing skills are not substantially advanced during the college years. I don't think this is coincidental. Despite rampant grade inflation, college dropout rates remain stubbornly high.[48]

Although there may be a correlation between the rise of financial aid and grade inflation, it is hard to see how aid causes grades to go up. Moreover, since aid rarely covers the full cost of attendance,

SAVING THE JOB MARKET?

it may be the failure of aid to prevent students from going into debt or working while in school that causes students to drop out.

There are many causes for grade inflation and few of them appear to be related to the use of financial aid. In fact, grades are another way that the free market myth of the invisible hand ends up creating a tragedy of the commons; in other words, when the free market logic is applied to education, the result is often a reduction of learning and student engagement. Like the quest to use technology to resolve all of the problems of higher education, the turn to the free market also represents a use of myths to avoid hard public policy decisions.

Notes

1 Giroux, Henry A. "Public pedagogy and the politics of neo-liberalism: Making the political more pedagogical." *Policy Futures in Education* 2.3 (2004): 494–503.
2 Taylor, Mark C. *Crisis on campus: A bold plan for reforming our colleges and universities.* Random House LLC, 2010.
3 Breneman, David W., Brian Pusser, and Sarah E. Turner, eds. *Earnings from learning: The rise of for-profit universities.* SUNY Press, 2012.
4 Mettler, Suzanne. *Degrees of inequality: How the politics of higher education sabotaged the American dream.* 2014.
5 Floyd, Carol Everly. "Know your competitor: Impact of for profit colleges on the higher education landscape." *New Directions for Higher Education* 2007.140 (2007): 121–129.
6 Gardner, Lee, and J. Young. "California's move toward MOOCs sends shock waves, but key questions remain unanswered." *The Chronicle of Higher Education* (2013).
7 Klein, Naomi. *The shock doctrine: The rise of disaster capitalism.* Macmillan, 2007.
8 Little Hoover Commission. *A new plan for a new economy: Reimagining higher education,* Report #218, October 2013: www.lhc.ca.gov/reports/listall.html.
9 Ibid.
10 Eagan, Kevin, et al. "The American freshman: National norms fall 2013." (2013): 8–9; www.usatoday.com/story/news/nation/2013/06/11/real-classrooms-better-than-virtual/2412401/.
11 Little Hoover.
12 Lewin, Tamar. "Professors at San Jose State Criticize Online Courses." *Ethnicity* 150 (2013): 2.
13 Little Hoover.

166 SAVING THE JOB MARKET?

14 Willging, Pedro A., and Scott D. Johnson. "Factors that influence students' decision to drop out of online courses." *Journal of Asynchronous Learning Networks* 13.3 (2009): 115–127.

15 Wellman, Jane V. "Spending more, getting less." *Change: The Magazine of Higher Learning* 40.6 (2008): 18–25.

16 Little Hoover.

17 Lepore, Jill. "The disruption machine: What the gospel of innovation gets wrong." *The New Yorker* (2014).

18 Ibid.

19 Little Hoover.

20 Lepore.

21 Ibid.

22 Ibid.

23 Ibid.

24 Ibid.

25 "How disruptive innovation is remaking the university": http://hbswk.hbs.edu/item/6746.html.

26 Ibid.

27 Ibid.

28 Ibid.

29 Koller, Daphne. "TED talk: What we are learning from online education." *URL: www.ted.com/talks/daphne_koller_what_we_re_learning_from_online_education.html* (2012).

30 Ibid.

31 Ibid.

32 Ibid.

33 Lewin, Tamar. "Professors at San Jose State criticize online courses." *Ethnicity* 150 (2013).

34 Koller.

35 Carnevale, Dan. "Employers often distrust online degrees." *Chronicle of Higher Education* 53.18 (2007): A28–A30.

36 Koller.

37 Ibid.

38 Ibid.

39 Ibid.

40 Ibid.

41 Puschmann, Cornelius, and Jean Burgess. "The politics of Twitter data." *Twitter and Society* 89 (2014): 43–54.

42 Koller.

43 Ibid.

44 "Changing the higher education system: Lowering costs, improving outcomes": http://centerforcollegeaffordability.org/2013/11/15/changing-the-higher-education-system-lowering-costs-improving-outcomes/.

45 Ibid.

46 Ibid.

47 Ibid.

48 Ibid.

CONCLUSION

EDUCATING EQUALITY

As I have argued throughout this book, fixing many of the problems regarding higher education will not do much good if we don't also begin to improve the employment structure. Producing more people with college degrees during a time when fewer jobs actually require this level of education is a recipe for underemployment, unemployment, and a decrease in wages. Some of the clearest solutions to this problem are making it easier for workers to unionize, increasing the Earned Income Tax Credit, raising the minimum wage, pursuing fair trade agreements, and creating government jobs to rebuild our crumbling infrastructure and create a green economy.[1] Many of these goals can be partially achieved through a change in our system of taxation. For example, in order to move businesses and individuals away from financial speculation and the hording of profits by managers, we can increase the capital gains tax above the top tax bracket. Likewise, we can eliminate all tax breaks and subsidies, in order to create a more fair and transparent system. It is estimated that tax breaks and subsidies cost the U.S. government two trillion dollars annually or one third of its yearly revenue.[2] However, this change can only work if we find a more effective way of fighting the offshoring of revenue for tax avoidance. By negotiating better international agreements regarding taxation, we can increase our revenue and help fund an increase in the Earned Income Tax Credit and unemployment insurance. These policies are necessary to stimulate the economy and increase consumer demand, which could also motivate businesses

168 EDUCATING EQUALITY

to hire more workers, especially if corporations no longer have the incentive to invest their reserves in financial speculation. Moreover, limiting executive pay to a certain percentage above the average workers' pay would incentivize companies to pay their workers more and put less money into stock buybacks that feed compensation at the top.[3]

Although it seems like these policies are too ideal, we must realize that many Northern European countries have successfully implemented most of these programs, and the result has been a reduction of inequality and increase in economic productivity.[4] Of course, one of the main things blocking these changes is the way we finance political campaigns. The current system is a form of legal bribery where politicians have to raise incredible sums of money from special interests to pay for superficial television commercials. Unfortunately, one reason why it is hard to change this system is that the Supreme Court has ruled that money equals speech, and since you cannot regulate speech, you also cannot regulate the money funding speech.[5] However, with the increased use of digital technology for media consumption, we may soon have a situation where most people do not watch political advertisements on television, and so free ads on the Web could undermine the structure where only the people who can raise the most amount of money can win elections. In fact, many recent elections have been won by people who were outspent, and so money does not guarantee a political victory; after all, the people still have to vote.[6]

Democracy and Capitalism

Perhaps the biggest challenge for the twenty-first century is how to balance democracy and capitalism. As our politics are taken over by the power of money, people are losing faith in the system. Meanwhile, our economy is becoming increasingly undemocratic. However, Stephen Hill documents in his *Europe's Promise* that countries like Germany, Sweden, Denmark, Finland, and Norway have been successful in achieving a better combination of democracy and capitalism by allowing for a high-level

EDUCATING EQUALITY

of workplace democracy.[7] For example, in Germany, not only are workers represented on the board of directors for large and small firms, but also the high rate of unionization gives workers a greater say in business and the political system. Moreover, Germany, like other Northern European countries, realizes that modern capitalism is very dynamic and disruptive, and so a strong safety net and system of retraining has to be available for displaced workers.

John Marsh has shown that even if we do a better job of increasing job and education opportunities in America, we still need programs that directly support people in poverty. Since so many workers today are living near or below the poverty line, producing more jobs is not the only solution. So far, the only thing that has been proven to work to bring people out of poverty in advanced economies is direct transfer of funds. In the United States, we have the Earned Income Tax Credit, and this program, along with food stamps and unemployment insurance, has helped to lift many people out of dire poverty, but much more needs to be done.[8]

In order to pursue many of the progressive policies that I have been discussing, we have to move beyond the myth that higher education is the solution to all of our economic and social problems. As I have shown, in our current system, higher education actually increases inequality, decreases social mobility, and does little to reduce poverty. Of course, some politicians like to focus on college as the solution to inequality because they have given up on the idea that the government can directly intervene in the job economy. After several decades of antigovernment rhetoric, we are seeing the emergence of a libertarian consensus that rejects the very idea that the government could improve job prospects and wages by simply hiring more teachers, health-care workers, and public servants. In fact, if we want to counter the current buyer's market for labor, which allows employers to set the terms and conditions for employment, we have to find a way of employing more educated workers, and the government can do this through the creation of more public-sector jobs. In fact, during and after the Great Recession, some of the largest job losses for middle-class employment occurred in the public sector after states were forced to cut their budgets and funding for education, health care, and public services, and these are precisely the jobs that are hard to automate and outsource.

One way, then, to increase the power of labor is to simply hire more public employees, and this has the further benefit of increasing the number of unionized employees. Of course, many people will reject this solution because they have been brought up in a political culture that demonizes public employees and organized labor. Like the myths of the fair meritocracy and the invisible hand, the myths surrounding unionized public workers have fed into an ideology that promotes the free market approach to labor. Instead of seeing how many stable middle-class jobs are the result of unionization and public-sector employment, people now feel that only private employers should be trusted with the creation of good jobs. However, what we have seen for decades is that many of the private-sector employers care mostly about increasing their profits and decreasing their labor costs, and so they have had no problem in outsourcing jobs to areas that deny union rights. In fact, as large corporations fund the campaigns of politicians who push through antilabor legislation, many voters continue to believe in the myth that only small businesses create jobs.

Of course, universities and colleges do not help with fighting the bad reputation of public institutions when they continue to raise the cost of attending their schools as they continue to build fancy dorms and entertainment centers. What we need is a new way of funding private and public universities directly so that they have an incentive to focus their attention on instruction and basic research. In fact, if we look at how we are currently spending our tax dollars on higher education, we will see that many of the programs are actually aid to the wealthy. For instance, in 2011–2012, it would have cost $195 billion to make all public community colleges and universities free to the students. Using national statistics, this total is derived from the following facts: there were 6.7 million full-time equivalent undergraduate

EDUCATING EQUALITY 171

students enrolled in public universities and 4.2 million enrolled in community colleges in 2011–2012, and the average cost of tuition, room, board, books, and living expenses for undergraduates at public four-year institutions was \$20,612, while at two-year public colleges, it was \$13,237.[9] Although \$195 billion is a lot of money, during the same period, we spent about \$201 billion on all types of aid and tax breaks related to higher education. Here is the breakdown:

\$35 Billion Pell Grants[10]
\$11 Billion State Financial Aid[11]
\$27 Billion Student Loan Subsidization[12]
\$40 Billion Federal Tax Breaks[13]
\$12 Billion Veteran Higher Ed Benefits[14]
@\$17 Billion 529 College Savings Plans[15]
@\$10 Billion State Tax Breaks (estimated)[16]
@\$40 Billion Institutional Aid and Tuition Discounting[17]
@\$10 Billion Federal and State Work Study Funding[18]

My plan is that instead of funding students through these different forms of aid, we fund the public institutions directly with the following requirements: the federal government would require states to maintain their current higher ed funding with inflation adjustments, 75% of student credit hours would have to be taught by full-time faculty, 75% of student credit hours generated in classes with less than 26 students, and 50% of tuition funding would go to direct instructional costs.

The idea behind this plan is to use current funding in a more coherent and effective manner by forcing colleges and universities to focus on their instructional missions and to make sure that their externally funded research projects do not have to be subsidized out of undergraduate funds. This plan would also improve the working conditions of many of the part-time faculty, and it would also reduce the reliance on ineffective large lecture classes. Instead of spending billions on subsidizing student loans and higher education tax breaks that often go to the

172   EDUCATING EQUALITY

wealthy, student loans would be eliminated and funding would be used for direct support for public institutions. This would also entail the end of support for for-profit colleges that used over $25 billion in federal aid in 2013. My plan would also eliminate costly work-study programs that make it hard for students to focus on their studies and graduate on a timely basis.

Making Higher Education More Democratic and Less Capitalistic

As I have argued throughout this book, not only do we have to change how we fund institutions of higher education, but we must also find ways to make schools more democratic and less focused on grading, ranking, and rating everything. For these changes to occur, we need a new conception of what education means and what really motivates people to work and learn. I have argued that grades act as form of rationed capital, and students learn from a very young age to only care about earning and not learning. In creating a system where everyone competes against everyone else for a scarce resource, we create a society of competitive capitalists who do not focus on the common good. Perhaps the most radical thing we can do to transform this culture is to simply eliminate grades and stop seeing education as an economic and social sorting system.

This radical suggestion will of course shock people and upset their preconceived notions of how contemporary society functions, but we have to realize that we are going through a new technological revolution that changes how knowledge is distributed and rewarded. In fact, one way of eliminating grades is to simply put most of a student's work online so that future employers or schools can judge for themselves the quality of a student's learning. Moreover, as many of my students have told me, they do not see the reason for memorizing information since they can just go online and find any knowledge that they need. To adjust to this situation, schools and colleges have to realize that the most important thing they can teach students is how to generate and interpret knowledge on their own as they also learn how to

EDUCATING EQUALITY 173

work with others through collaborative projects. Unfortunately, I have found that when I do have students engage in group work, they often complain because they do not want to have their individual grade lowered because some other student did not do a good job. However, if we get rid of grades, we can undermine this individualistic approach to learning and work.

Grades not only socialize students to be amoral competitors, but the focus on getting a good grade often pushes the students to memorize what they think the teacher will put on the test. Therefore, instead of developing creative and critical thinking skills, students focus on how to game the system and how to memorize and then forget information. What we need to do instead is to eliminate large lecture classes and standardized tests and teach students in small, interactive courses. Although people think this would be a very expensive proposition, I have found that small classes taught by secure full-time faculty (with or without tenure) can be less expensive than giant courses that require many sections taught by graduate student instructors. Furthermore, even if this type of education is more expensive, it is worth it because large classes often train students to be undemocratic passive consumers of fragmented information.

Perhaps the most important lesson of this book is that universities and colleges have to stop trying to be the solution to all social and economic problems because if they are the solution, they are also the problem. Moreover, when schools stop focusing on their basic mission of helping people learn more about the world around them, they take on many other costly functions and have no way of controlling their costs. Institutions of higher education should not see their missions as indoctrinating students into a particular ideology or training them for specific jobs; instead, colleges and universities have to focus on providing a space for the objective and unbiased analysis of knowledge and society. While objectivity and neutrality may be impossible ideals, it is still necessary to pursue truth through learning and research.

As a public good, universities and colleges should create a space outside of the dominating structures of neoliberal capitalism.

174 EDUCATING EQUALITY

Of course, these schools need to be funded, and they have to be careful how they spend their resources, but they should not be selling their research to the highest bidder or engaging in activities just to bring in more money. As training grounds for democratic citizenship, these institutions have to create a culture of cooperation and participation and not one of competition and selfish greed. Through a focus on pursing knowledge for knowledge's sake, an ethic of honesty and openness has to be promoted, and this means changing the way we structure education and talk about the common good.

We have to face the fact that one reason why an undemocratic amoral capitalist has been able to reach the highest level of power in the "free world" is that our education system trains people to be competitive individualists who are not able to participate in shaping the world around them. Trump is not only the logical extension of educational socialization, but he is also the product of a misunderstanding regarding the relations among degrees, jobs, and inequality. People believe that it is primarily the "uneducated" who voted for him; however, many people with college degrees did support him. Moreover, as school is currently structured, there is no reason to think that it makes people more just or fair; in fact, I have been arguing that education in America today educates people to tolerate high levels of inequality as they compete for a dwindling number of good jobs.

Although Trump wants people to believe that immigrants and bad trade deals have undermined the U.S. economy, the truth is that individual corporations have decided that they do not have a responsibility to provide workers with fair wages or secure jobs, and in a globalized, automating economy, multinational corporations will seek out the lowest labor costs in order to increase their profits. Due in part to the massive decrease in unionization, workers have lost their bargaining power, and as more and more workers compete internationally for the same jobs, a global buyer's market for labor has been established. The only real solution is to realize that since we have a global economy, we now need a global system of justice and governance. Just as companies and

EDUCATING EQUALITY

wealthy individuals can move their profits around the world to avoid paying taxes, multinational corporations not only search the globe for the cheapest workers, but they also seek out the places with the fewest regulations and labor protections. In this global race to the bottom, individual countries are no longer able to control the flow of money, labor, and consumption: we need a global system for a globalized economy.

It is also important to stress that global climate change cannot be reversed by just a few countries since we all share the same environment. Likewise, global poverty and inequality affect everyone since they cause mass migration and a depression of global consumption. Instead of building walls and expelling immigrants, we have to realize that we are all in this together. In fact, the global financial crisis of 2008 should have taught us that a missed loan payment in California can cause a town in Iceland to lay off its public employees. In other words, we are all connected now, and the age of the nation-state is becoming a thing of the past.

Perhaps we can turn to public universities to help us think about how we need to structure our political and social institutions to deal with the new global order. Instead of thinking in terms of the competition between nations, we should begin to think about the roles and values of a global community. While I have tried not to make many predictions in this book, I want to close by arguing that if we want to save our planet and our lives, we are going to have to start building a global democratic government that can support all people and protect everyone's human rights. We therefore need a broader vision for public education that moves beyond borders by promoting universal equality and global awareness.

Notes

1 Most of these proposals are discussed in Stiglitz, Joseph. *The price of inequality*. Penguin UK, 2012: 266–290.

2 www.cbo.gov/publication/42919.

3 Hribar, Paul, Nicole Thorne Jenkins, and W. Bruce Johnson. "Stock repurchases as an earnings management device." *Journal of Accounting and Economics* 41.1 (2006): 3–27.

4 See Stephen Hill's *Europe's promise.*
5 Smith, Bradley A. "Money talks: Speech, corruption, equality, and campaign finance." *Geo. LJ* 86 (1997): 45.
6 www.outsidethebeltway.com/money-cant-buy-elections-after-all/.
7 Hill, 62–65.
8 Eissa, Nada, and Hilary Williamson Hoynes. "Taxes and the labor market participation of married couples: The earned income tax credit." *Journal of Public Economics* 88.9 (2004): 1931–1958.
9 Sources: http://nces.ed.gov/programs/digest/d13/tables/dt13_330.10. asp. http://nces.ed.gov/programs/digest/d12/tables/dt12_288.asp.
10 Turner, Lesley J. "The incidence of student financial aid: Evidence from the Pell Grant program." *Columbia University, Department of Economics* (2012): 91.
11 Sjoquist, David L., and John V. Winters. *State merit-based financial aid programs and college attainment.* No. 6801. Discussion paper series, Forschungsinstitut zur Zukunft der Arbeit, 2012.
12 Avery, Christopher, and Sarah Turner. "Student loans: Do college students borrow too much—or not enough?." *The Journal of Economic Perspectives* (2012): 165–192.
13 Pew Charitable Trusts. "Tax expenditures in the education sector": www.pewtrusts.org/~/media/legacy/uploadedfiles/pcs_assets/2012/Subsidyscope_Education_Sector.pdf.
14 Baum, Sandy, and Kathleen Payea. "Trends in student aid 2013." *Trends in Higher Education Series.* New York: College Board, 2013; https://trends.collegeboard.org/sites/default/files/student-aid-2013-full-report-140108.pdf.
15 Burd, Stephen. "Moving on up": www.educationsector.org/publications/moving-how-tuition-tax-breaks-increasingly-favor-upper-middle-class.
16 Corporation for Enterprise Development. "Upside down: Higher education tax spending." http://cfed.org/assets/pdfs/Upside_Down_-_Higher_Education_Tax_Expenditures.pdf.
17 Baum, Sandy, and Kathleen Payea. "Trends in student aid 2013." *Trends in Higher Education Series.* New York: College Board, 2013. https://trends.collegeboard.org/sites/default/files/student-aid-2013-full-report-140108.pdf.
18 Ibid.

INDEX

academic freedom 119
academic labor 119
administration xii, 89, 115, 119, 121, 122, 123, 146, 163–64
admission policies 47, 49–50, 55–56, 68, 70, 108–09, 122
Affordable Care Act, the 41
Alexander, Lamar 38–39, 52
Armstrong, Elizabeth and Laura Hamilton 108–14, 116
austerity 74–76, 86–87, 95, 143, 153
automation 21–22, 59
Autor, David 23
Avery, Christopher, and Sarah Turner 176

Baker, Dean 34
Baum, Sandy and Kathleen Payea 176
behavioral economics 126
Belous, Richard S. 34
Benjamin, Ernst 116
Bewley, Truman F. 35
binge drinking 113
Birdsall, Nancy 67
Blanden, Joe, Paul Gregg, and Stephen Machin 34
Bluestone, Barry, and Bennett Harrison 10
Blundell, Richard 67
Bousquet, Marc 34, 44–45,
Bracher, Mark 7, 11

Breneman, David W., Brian Pusser, and Sarah E. Turner 165
Budd, Mike 34
Burd, Stephen 52, 54, 176
Bush, George W. 7, 58
buyer's labor market 13–19, 22, 27, 29, 32, 169

Cabrera, Alberto F., and Steven M. La Nasa 33
Caldwell, Raymond 67
California 143–47, 149
capitalism 74, 76, 81, 83–84, 86, 90, 106, 121, 123, 124–25, 127, 130, 133, 168–69, 172, 173–74
careerism 121
Carnegie, Andrew 1–2
Carr, Neil 52
Charette, Robert N. 34
Chemerinsky, Erwin 136
Christensen, Clayton and Henry Eyring 151–52
Clancy, Patrick, and Gaële Goastellec 136
class hierarchies 109–10, 114–15
Clawson, Dan 34
Clinton, Bill 4, 9, 11
Colander, David 67
college premium, the 12–13, 23–25, 30, 62–63, 68, 69
college rankings xii, 8, 55–56, 57, 65, 68, 70, 103, 104, 123, 125, 172
Collinge, Alan 53

INDEX

conformity 72
Congressional Budget Office, the 41
conservatives 8, 73, 74, 78, 118, 119, 120, 121, 126, 129
contingent faculty (see also nontenure-track faculty and part-time faculty) 14–15, 123
Cosmides, Leda, and John Tooby 137, 141
Cowan, Tyler 61
critical thinking xii, 10, 60, 85, 88, 101, 106–07, 108, 109, 110, 115, 118, 123, 158, 173
Critical University Studies xiii
Cude, Brenda 52
cynical conformity 9–10, 65, 66, 89, 95, 96, 99, 101, 102–07, 112, 115, 120, 125, 144

Davidson, Cathy N. 131–35, 140, 141
Davies, Scott, and Neil Guppy 33
debt collectors 41–42
degree attainment x, 4, 12, 19, 32, 37, 44, 48, 50, 56, 146
de-industrialization 3
Delisle, Jason 53
democracy 33, 64, 76, 94, 101, 102, 105, 106, 108, 115, 118, 119, 134, 168–69, 172, 174–75
Democrats xii, 4, 32, 39, 105, 119, 121
Descartes, René 105, 116
Dewey, John 76
D'Souza, Dinesh 136
Durand, Rodolphe, and Vicente Vargas 141

Eagan, Kevin 165
Eissa, Nada, and Hilary Williamson Hoynes 176
Elbow, Peter 67
elite colleges and universities 30, 68, 71, 72, 82, 93, 96, 154, 162
Elman, Cheryl, and M. O. Angela 34

evolutionary psychology 126–29, 133, 135
expertise 101, 134, 148, 160
external rewards 6–7, 66, 74–81, 84–99

FASFA 47
Feldstein, Martin 10
female students 50, 113, 115
financial aid x, xi, xii, 33, 37–51, 111, 112, 162–65
financialization 30, 167–68
Floyd, Carol Everly 165
for-profit college xii, 40, 46–47, 50, 142–43
Frank, Thomas 10, 62–63, 67, 136
free labor 134, 149, 158,
free market xii, 9, 130–33, 135, 136, 142–43, 160, 161, 162–65, 170
free trade 59–60
Freire, Paulo 137
fraternities and sororities 109–10

Gardner, Lee, and J. Young 165
Gates, Bill 12
Germany xi, 20, 168–69
Gillen, Andrew 52
Ginsberg, Benjamin 34
Giroux, Henry A. 122–26, 137, 165
Gladieux, Lawrence, and Laura Perna 52
globalization 3, 4, 19, 59–61, 174–75
Goldrick-Rab, S., and Sorenson, K. 54
Goodfriend, Marvin 35
grading xii, 7, 8, 56, 65–66, 81, 84–85, 87–88, 89–99, 102, 104, 106, 115, 123, 124–26, 132, 158–59, 164–65, 172–73
graduate students 15, 45, 120, 121, 122, 158–59, 173
graduation rates x
Great Recession, the 22–23, 27, 30, 76, 94, 133, 143, 170
Greene, Jay P., and Greg Forster 36

INDEX

179

Greenspan, Alan 133
Grolnick, Wendy 79–80
Grusky, David B., Bruce Western, and Christopher Wimer 36

Haseltine, Eric 137
Harvard University 114, 144, 151, 152
Havrilesky, Heather 69–73, 99
Hayek, Friedrich August 130, 132, 140
Hayes, Christopher 63–66, 67
Hedges, Chris 120–21, 137
high-income (rich, wealthy) 29–30, 37, 42, 43, 44–47, 48, 49, 50, 56, 68, 75, 91, 94, 109, 111–12, 142, 162
Higher education Act 38
Hill, Stephen 168, 176
Horowitz, David 137
Hribar, Paul, Nicole Thorne Jenkins, and W. Bruce Johnson 165
human capital 59

IMF 76
inequality x, xi, 1, 3–4, 5, 8, 9, 23–24, 29, 31, 37, 40, 43, 45–47, 49, 50–51, 55, 57–58, 61, 63, 68, 69, 74, 91, 95, 102, 109, 118, 112, 123, 127, 129, 131, 132, 136, 142, 175
invisible hand, the 6, 7, 103, 130–31, 133, 150, 159, 161, 163
irony 125

Jacobs, Jerry A., and Kathleen Green 35
job market xiii, 3, 12–13, 15–28, 32, 50, 51, 59, 165
Johnson, Lyndon 2

K-12 xi, 31, 45, 49, 71, 77, 89–99, 105–06, 111, 125
Kahlenberg, Richard 49–50, 54
Kaku, Michio 137

Kaufman, Bruce 140
Keller, George 36
Kezar, Adrianna J., and John Burkhardt 11, 136
Kirkham, Chris 54
Kirp, David 34, 137
Klein, Naomi 165
Kocherlakota, Narayana 20–21
Kohn, Alfie 73–89, 99
Koller, Daphne 154–162, 166
Kraus, Michael W., and Dacher Keltner 66
Kristof, Nicholas 58
Krugman, Paul 10
Kurtz, Howard 136

Labaree, David F. 66, 105–06, 108, 116
labor exploitation 122, 123, 132
Lach, Alex 66
Lafer, Gordon 34
large lecture classes xii, 85, 101, 104, 122, 171, 173
Left, the 10, 32, 64, 73, 118, 123, 125, 142
Lepore, Jill 148–50, 166
Levy, Ariel 117
Lewin, Tamar 53, 165
liberals xii, 11, 40, 78, 118, 119–23, 125–27, 129, 131, 132, 150
libertarian xii, 8, 9, 118, 129–33, 135–36, 142, 150, 159, 169
Linsenmeier, David M., Harvey S. Rosen, and Cecilia Elena Rouse 54
Little Hoover Commission 144–47, 149, 165, 166
Logue, A. W. 140
Loonin, Deanne, and Jillian McLaughlin 53
lottery economy 13
low-income 3, 30–31
low-income students, 30–31, 37, 39–40, 44, 45, 47, 48–49, 98, 143, 163

180 INDEX

low-wage workers 26–28, 60–61, 143
Lynch, Mamie, Jennifer Engle, and
    José L. Cruz 52
Lythcott-Haims, Julie 69–73

Magill Jr, R. Jay 137
managers 14–15
Marsh, John 1–6, 10, 11, 58, 59, 61,
    66, 67, 169
McGilchrist, Iain 141
McKinsey & Company 34
mental health 80, 90, 93–94
merit aid 43, 47, 56
meritocracy xi, xiii, 5–7, 55–66,
    73, 74–75, 78, 80, 87–88, 90,
    95, 103, 105, 111, 124, 131,
    142, 154
Mettler, Suzanne 36, 39–40, 43–44,
    51, 52, 53, 54, 165
middle-class x, 3, 27–29, 32, 40, 47,
    48, 68, 70–72, 80, 82–83, 170
military financial aid 46
Miller, John and Jeannettte
    Wicks-Lim 25–27, 35
minority students 49, 82, 96
Mishel, Lawrence 21–25, 35
mismatch theory of labor 20–25, 26
MOOCs 135, 143, 147, 151, 154–162
Monden, Yasuhiro 34
Murphy, Kevin, and Finis Welch 34

NAFTA 4
narcissism 65
Nathan, Rebekah 107–08, 116
neoliberalism 8, 75–80, 82, 83,
    86–88, 90, 95, 121, 122–24,
    142, 143, 145–46, 148–50, 152,
    153, 173–74
neuroscience 126, 127–29, 133, 135
New York Federal Reserve 42, 53
Newfield Chris 137
Nisbet, Robert A. 121, 137
non-tenure-track faculty 64, 109,
    119, 123
Northern Europe xi, 20, 168–69

Obama, Barak 7, 16, 25, 27, 31–32,
    36, 52, 55, 59, 63–64
online education xii, 46, 131,
    142, 135, 143–47, 149, 151,
    154–162

parenting xi, xiii, 68–83
part-time faculty 15, 23, 26, 45, 46,
    61, 120, 121, 122, 123, 143,
    146, 149, 171
Peck, Jamie, Nik Theodore, and
    Neil Brenner 99
Pell Grants 39–40, 48
Petersen, Michael Bang, et al. 140
Piff, Paul 57, 66
Piketty, Thomas 36
Pinker, Steven 129, 140
Pope, Denise Clark 89–99, 100
poverty 1–3, 19, 30, 58–59, 169, 175
Power, Mark, Carlo Bonifazi, and
    Kevin C. Desouza 11
private good xiii, 5, 32–33, 40–41,
    62, 68, 78, 105, 121, 142, 143,
    145, 150–51
private universities 40, 47, 49, 152,
    175
public good xi, xiii, 5, 8, 32–33,
    40–41, 62, 68, 78, 105–06, 121,
    125, 142, 143, 145, 150–51
public universities 40–41, 49,
    109–12, 121, 161, 170–71
public sector jobs 19, 169, 170
Puschmann, Cornelius, and Jean
    Burgess 166
Putnam, Robert D. 11

Rampell, Catherine 35, 66
Rand, Ayn 133
Ravitch, Diane 31, 36, 53
Reagan, Ronald 9
Republicans xii, 4, 39
research 121
Reuss, Alejandro 35
Right, the 10, 32, 64, 73, 122,
    125, 142

INDEX

181

Roland-Holst, David, Kenneth A. Reinert, and Clinton R. Shiells 11
Runcie, James W. 39
Ryan, Richard M., and Edward L. Deci 11

SAT x–xi, 43, 56, 103, 111
Satel, Sally, and Scott O. Lilienfeld 137
Samuels, Robert 51, 54, 115
San Jose State University 156
sexism 109, 113, 115
sexual assault 112–13
Shriver, Sargent 2
Silverman, Jacob 115
Singell Jr, Larry D., and Joe A. Stone 52, 53
Sjoquist, David L., and John V. Winters 176
Sloterdijk, Peter 115
Smith, Adam 130
Smith, Bradley A. 176
Soares, Louis 141
social Darwinism 6, 7, 9, 74, 95, 123, 126–29, 131, 133, 142, 144–45, 148, 153, 163
social hierarchy 125–26, 129, 134,
social mobility x, 1, 5, 20, 40, 42, 47, 50–51, 55, 61, 68, 92, 105, 111, 154
Social Network, The 114–15
social trust 8, 9–10, 78, 91
Sperber Murray 110, 115
STEM degrees x, 15–19
STEM jobs x, 15–19, 32
Stiglitz, Joseph 11, 53, 99, 165
student debt ix, 10, 39–40, 41–42, 45, 48, 143, 172
student evaluations 109, 115
Surowiecki, James 140

Tallis, Raymond 138–40
tax policy 4, 20, 31, 37, 43, 45–46, 50, 60, 75, 167–69, 171, 175

Taylor, Mark C. 165
tenure 14–15, 46, 64, 122, 123
Terranova, Tiziana 140
The Matrix 116
Tooby, John 127
Toomcy, Traci L., and Alexander C. Wagenaar 117
Toren, Nina 35
total cost of attendance 38–39, 41, 43, 48
tragedy of the commons, the 68, 105–06
Trump, Donald 148, 174
tuition xii, 38–39, 41, 43, 50–51, 162–64, 171
Turner, Lesley J. 176

UC Berkeley 152
undemocratic capitalists xii, 77, 101
undergraduate education
underemployment x, 15, 17–29, 32, 59, 143, 159, 167
unemployment 7, 19, 21–26, 28, 32, 33, 42, 59, 132, 159, 167
unionization 1, 4, 5, 20, 121, 170
United States xi, 8, 15–19, 59, 123, 167–69
University of California 152
U.S. Bureau of Labor 16–17
U.S. Commerce Department 16–17
U.S. Department of Education 39
U.S. Department of Labor 25–26
US News and World Report 43, 70, 103
U.S. Senate Committee on Health, Education, Labor, and Pensions 38

Vedder, Richard 35, 162–164

wages vs. productivity 4, 29, 75
Walpole, MaryBeth 53
Warren, Elizabeth 52
Washburn, Jennifer 136

INDEX

Watters, Audrey 141
Web, the 130–36
Wechsler, Henry 117
welfare 33, 49, 58, 75, 76, 128–29
Wellman, Jane V. 166
Willging, Pedro A., and Scott D.
    Johnson 165
Wilkinson, Richard, and Kate
    Pickett 8, 11
Williams, Jeffrey 53

World Bank, the 76
work-study 44, 172
Working America 60

Young, Michael Dunlop 66

Žižek, Slavoy 104, 116
Zucker, Gail Sahar, and Bernard
    Weiner 10,
Zuckerberg, Mark 114–15